When Death Comes

WHEN DEATH COMES

William G. Justice

BROADMAN PRESS
Nashville, Tennessee

© Copyright 1982 • BROADMAN PRESS.
All rights reserved.

4269-37
ISBN: 0-8054-6937-0

Dewey Decimal Classification: 242.4
Subject heading: DEATH

Library of Congress Catalog Card Number: 81-68365
Printed in the United States of America

To
the memory of
William Gross Justice, Sr.
who taught me
about fathering,
by fathering
about loving,
by loving
about work,
by working
about play,
by playing
about grief,

by dying.

And he'll probably have some interesting observations
about the resurrection, too.

Blessed are they that mourn:
for they shall be comforted.
Matthew 5:4

Jesus said . . . I am the resurrection, and the life: he
that believeth in me, though he were dead, yet shall
he live.
John 11:25

. . . So shall we ever be with the Lord.
. . . Comfort one another with these words.
1 Thessalonians 4:17-18

CONTENTS

Preface

"How can I have a richer ministry to families when there's been a death?" That is one of the questions closest to the minister's heart. Having lectured and led discussion groups for more than twenty years on various subjects related to pastoral care of the sick and otherwise distressed, I have heard no question raised more often by pastors and ministering laymen.

These are the persons to whom this book primarily is addressed, but doctors and nurses should acquaint themselves with the ideas of chapters 1, 2, and 3. In few instances do I speak only to the pastor, and that is done while discussing the funeral practices that have been (to my experience) assigned by custom or church policy to the ordained gospel minister.

This book, then, is for the "minister"—any person in the Christian ministering role who has heard the call to serve our Lord Jesus Christ by serving those wounded by the loss of a loved one. But the basics are here for *anyone* who works with the grieving.

If you ask that "typical man on the street" to define grief for you, almost without exception you will hear something comparable to, "Grief is what you *feel* when somebody you love dies." While the word generally has been reserved for feelings concerning death, we should remember that the loss of *anything* we love arouses many similar feelings. While in this book I am discussing ministry to those whose loss has been by death, keep your mind open to the implications for a much wider ministry. If you will reflect a few moments, you will real-

11

ize that at least three-fourths of your ministry to persons in distress is needed because of some *loss.* One person will have lost a loved one, another his job, and another the family pet. (Take that seriously. People can invest much of themselves in their pets.) Another may have lost his health, his dream, his hope, his leg, or his self-respect. You can name more. Each loss produces a form of grief. Much of the material here can be applied to our ministry amid any loss.

No one person can minister to all the hurt in any church. It takes a team. If you are not already a part of such a team, is it possible that you should become a part of one—even if you have to begin it yourself? Of course, it takes preparation.

Of the hundreds of books on the subject of pastoral care that line our shelves, most are good. Some are excellent. But almost all deal with abstract ideas. (And they have been needed!) I have chosen here to address the concrete, specific needs of the grieving, and the concrete, specific ways the minister can help meet those needs.

After my book *Don't Sit on the Bed,* A Handbook for Visiting the Sick (Broadman, 1973) was published, the renowned writer and teacher Wayne E. Oates congratulated me for having had the "courage to say the obvious." It dealt with the concrete "do's" and "don'ts" of visiting the sick. The public response to that work has clearly indicated a need for the concrete, "Do this and don't do that," mechanical approach to some of our ministry. Even the obvious sometimes needs to be said.

Two rules have governed my efforts to produce this body of material. First, it had to be practical. Second, everything had to be said in plain language. To reassure myself and the reader that I had accomplished those intents, I submitted an earlier draft of this material to several persons with differing backgrounds for their critical evaluations.

Jennie Leland, "Katie" Webb, and Ann Justice (my wife) offered a lay perspective. Chaplains Paul Bay, Mark Gaines (my associates), and Charles Burrows (Lakeland General

Hospital, Lakeland, Florida) gave suggestions from their professional viewpoint. The Reverends James Hudson (my pastor), Gay Harris (retired after having served as a pastor for forty-two years and as a chaplain to a chain of funeral homes for three years), and Filmore Strunk (pastor, Central Baptist Church, Oak Ridge, Tennessee, with *fifty* of the best trained, church-wide appreciated, ministering deacons I have ever seen) responded from the experienced pastor's view. And Laird Bryson, MD (heart specialist) reacted from his perspective as a physician. Each have my genuine gratitude. Additional thanks go to Mrs. Winnie Lamb who took my ugly stack of white and yellow, marked, clipped, and glued papers and turned them into an attractive typescript.

1

There's Been a Death

The phone rings. You fumble in the dark as it rings again, and you note that it's 2:15 AM. Your head's not clear, but you are afraid you may have heard correctly. "Say that again."

"Mr. Fred Jackson was in a head-on collision out on the bypass a while ago. It looks bad. Mrs. Jackson is on her way to the emergency room of our hospital. She's going to need somebody. If there's any way for you to be here before she arrives, we'd sure appreciate it."

"Yeah. As soon as I can get dressed, I'll be on my way."

You splash cold water in your face, glance in the mirror, and wish you'd shaved before you went to bed. You hurriedly throw on a suit, adjusting your tie as you go out the back door.

Even as you start the car, phrases are echoing. "Emergency room . . . be here before she arrives." You tell yourself that the urgency of the situation justifies your violation of the speed limit, at least a little. Besides, it's too early for many cars to be on the street.

Settled under the steering wheel, phrases come again. It's the first time you have had time to reflect. ". . . Head-on collision. . . . It looks bad." *It sounds as though Fred may not live. What will Helen do? They've got three small children. Tommy, the oldest, can't be more than nine.* You know them well—since they moved here just after they married ten years ago—*or was it eleven? But that's not important.*

What are you going to do? What are you going to say? Surely you were supposed to have learned that in the seminary or in that special training program you attended. But if anybody ever said anything about events like this, it must have been one of those times you had to miss class. *Inadequate.* That's the word. You don't like the sound of it, but that's the word that keeps ringing in your ears. *What can I do? What will I be able to say that doesn't sound completely empty? Why did I ever accept this kind of a responsibility in the first place?* You may be tempted to turn and go back, but you do care and you know God has helped you before in rough spots. And it *is* your responsibility. As you wheel into the emergency room parking lot, you note that the ambulance is still backed up to the door. You don't see Helen's car. Maybe you have been able to beat her here.

You introduce yourself to the nurse at the desk and ask about Fred. *Did she say DOA?* "What does that mean?" You see her lips moving, and you pick up the word "expired." *Oh! Dead On Arrival. No! Not Fred. He's too . . .* Before you finish your thought you see Helen coming through the door. Your "Oh Lord!" may be said more in desperation than in a quick prayer. Now it's up to you.

And that's often the way it is. It's up to you. Do your praying in advance, because you may have little time for it amid the crisis. You accepted a ministry, but you may have had no idea of how difficult it could become. All the ministry can't be left up to the Holy Spirit. God has called you to minister, too. Fred is dead because of a wreck. Sue's battle with cancer can't last much longer. She's got three small children, too. And Kate Thompson's father just committed suicide yesterday morning. Marge said that Tom probably wouldn't last more than another day or two. And you are going to have to try to minister to all of those who are left behind. Sometimes they all seem to come at once.

Yours is a ministry of reconciliation in which you strive to bring people to be at peace with God, to be at peace with the people important to their world, and to be at peace with themselves. You are not alone, but you are the person on the spot.

And "on the spot" may accurately describe your feelings.

You know you are going to have to minister, but how effective are you going to be? Your deepest fear may be that you may fail to be the person you want to be to those who need you.

God has called you to serve him by serving other people—people he loves and cares for just as much as he does you. The quality of your service is going to depend largely on what you know, what you do, what you say (or don't say), and what you are to them. You have watched others. You have read what you hoped would help. You have prayed that God would grant you the wisdom to use it all effectively. But then when you follow in the footsteps of tragedy you may feel you carry an empty bucket. And *that* is the feeling that can wipe you out!

I am personally convinced that the feeling of emptiness, of inadequacy, and of futility are the greatest paralyzers of ministry that we face. I suspect it to be the greatest cause of "ministerial dropout" and the strongest reason people have for saying no when called on to serve.

Since this just may be the biggest problem we face, let's get it up front and deal with it immediately. Consider the kinds of tragedy some people have to face. Who is completely adequate to minister when a twenty-five-year-old husband and father learns that he is forever paralyzed from the neck down? Nothing but his head can ever move again. When a ten-year-old boy learns that his mother and father and two sisters have just died when their home burned, tell me who is adequate to minister to him? Tell me of somebody's adequacy to minister to a young mother who sits in a daze, looking as though she has been dipped in a vat of blood after her only child bled to death in her arms on the way to the hospital.

Forgive me. I'm not trying to make you sick. I'm trying to make a point. *No human being is fully adequate to meet the needs of people who hurt amid life's great tragedies!* If you can accept that one truth you have made one giant step toward more effectively ministering amid major crises. Maybe you cannot accept that now. But the sooner you walk into the midst of tragedy that is so overwhelming you are forced to realize *no one* could possibly meet the needs, the better off you are going to be.

So you cannot meet all the needs. Are you going to walk away? Maybe. That's what a lot of people do. But I hope and pray that you will try to give the best you have. If you met a starving man and all you had was hamburger, would you walk away because you had no steak? So you don't have what you think might be the very best to give. Give of what you have until you can acquire something better. Who knows? That person in need just may grow on what you have to offer. You see, no one else may give either.

How much do you think you are going to minister anyway? Is it possible that Christ might minister through you? I'm not speaking in some terribly vague, abstract term. God often ministers most effectively through people!

Reflect with me on the following experience. A nurse called to tell me that Mr. Franklin's wife was in surgery and that they had just discovered cancer that probably would be fatal within a matter of weeks. Mr. Franklin had just been informed and was terribly upset. Would I come to talk with him? When I arrived, he sat with his face buried in his hands. Tears dripped from his knuckles. I introduced myself and sat down beside him in silence.

In a little while he wiped away the tears and began to tell me of the sad news about his wife. He went on to tell me of their more than thirty years of life together. He wandered through memories and recalled their joys and sorrows, their failures and their victories, their hopes and the fears they had shared. After having listened silently, for nearly an hour, giving only an occasional nod of the head or an "Uh-huh," I stood, assured him that I would remember him and his wife when I prayed, and I left.

The next day as I walked down the hall with a friend, I met

Mr. Franklin and asked about his wife. He told me of the latest developments and then turned to my friend. "The chaplain here will never know how much he helped me yesterday with all he had to say. Everything he said was just what I needed to hear." I was astonished. He was really serious. Later I began to wonder, *Who did speak to him?* My conclusion has been strengthened across the years after numerous similar experiences. Somebody's doing some talking, and I'm being given the credit for it. I'm convinced it is the Holy Spirit of God. I'm convinced that he spoke so clearly and loudly to Mr. Franklin amid his need that he seemed to have heard a human voice. Since I had the privilege of being there, he assumed it was I who spoke. Is it not truly possible that the Spirit of God actually ministers through human personality? The Scriptures clearly speak of the Christian being "in Christ" and Christ being in the Christian. Paul said, "I live; yet not I, but Christ liveth in me" (Gal. 2:20). Where no mere human being is adequate, *God* is adequate.

This is not to offer any excuse for ignorance. I see evidence that even God has a difficult time using an empty vessel. I've been supervising ministers in training, reading their own reports of their ministry too long to believe that the uninformed typically minister as effectively as the informed. I am urging for both a Christian commitment *and* thorough preparation. But there will still be many crises in which no one is *fully* adequate to minister. Note the emphasis on the word *fully*. It's not that we only *feel* inadequate. We *are* inadequate. Able to meet some needs? Yes. Able to meet *all* needs? No.

The dilemma begins with the familiar feeling of helplessness. What can I do? Much of the time we quickly realize there is absolutely nothing we can *do*. When someone is highly upset, after we have offered a box of tissue and a glass of water or a cup of coffee, what can we do? Usually nothing. When we can't help by "doing" we are likely to try to help by "saying." After all, we are there to help aren't we? But we may face the sickening awareness that even our words seem inadequate in the face of great pain. Again, it is not just a *feeling* of inadequacy. We *are* inadequate.

If you can accept this fact, among other things, you may not say a lot that creates problems. Look at two common statements people make as they approach the grieving. "I don't know what to say." Period—end of comment. And "I'm sorry." Again a comment is left hanging. *Both comments are self-centered.* Both comments give Helen an extra burden. In addition to the burden of her grief, she is given the burden of trying to figure out how to respond to *your* feelings. A good general rule to follow is: "If you don't know what to say, don't say it."

When you are lost for words, watch how easily the mouth seems to move faster than the mind. Beware of mouthing religious clichés. Remember that Job's friends sat with him, supporting him in absolute silence for seven days and seven nights (Job 2:11-13). Then they spoke and ruined it all by what they said.[1]

You might also ask yourself why you are about to speak. Is it truly for Helen's benefit or to satisfy some need within yourself? Or do you feel that some observer expects something of you? Judgments and hollow platitudes seem to come out when we feel we are expected to say something profound but worthwhile words evade us. If you can get comfortable with your discomfort, you may say less and listen more. Rely on your "ministry of listening."

You may be thinking, *But I've got to say something.* All right. If you arrive and find Helen is upset, you might ask, "What happened?" Or state something comparable to, "It must be pretty bad." If you know what has happened, and *you know* she knows, you might say something like, "I just heard the bad news. You've got to be hurting." Note that the suggested possible introductory comments have one characteristic in common. *They provide an immediate opportunity for her to speak of her husband or herself.* Either way, your feelings are left out, and her feelings are likely to surface immediately.

Listen carefully to the questions people ask when they are hurting. People don't really expect us to answer them when they ask "Why?" in the midst of their tears. On numerous occasions, amid some great tragedy, I've heard the "Why?" question raised. I have sometimes responded, "Do you really expect me to try to answer your question?" The usual type of response has been, "Not really, Chaplain. You'd probably just say something dumb and empty. And no matter how valuable it might be, I doubt that I'm in the mental condition to hear or understand it. Thanks for just sitting and listening to the stuff that's going through my mind." A personal friend and professional associate experienced the sudden, tragic death of a child. He says those who were the most help were "comfortable with their uncomfortableness" enough to listen quietly to the struggle within his soul.

When we listen attentively, we are often ushered into that person's most holy of holy places. It is the quiet closet to which normally only God has access. They may be looking at you, but often they are talking to God. The verbal expressions of their struggles may not be introduced with "Our Father which art in heaven" (Matt. 6:9), but they are in prayer. You don't normally intrude into someone's prayer. Don't do so now. Since prayer is a two-way communication, God just may have some better answers to their struggles than we do.

Having been taught they should *never* "question God," many feel a strong sense of guilt any time they ask, "Why, God?" Has God granted us intelligence and the sense of curiosity with which to ponder all other things except that which brings us pain? Surely not! Was man not supposed to bow reverently before God and ask, "Why, God? Why are our children being crippled or killed by the disease of polio?" And when men (maybe with the leadership of God) used their minds to find the cause, they were then able to find the cure.

God answers prayer! When we ask "Why," we sometimes may learn why. In fact, we may find a highly human "why." Abuse or neglect of one's own body or some other person's careless-ness is often the clear answer.

Be alert to any tendency to toss out pious clichés and easy answers to profound questions. These pat answers have a remarkable way of resulting in making God a part of the prob-lem instead of making him a part of the solution. Note the frequency with which God gets the blame for a tragedy. A drunk fails to stop at a stop sign and plows into a man on his way home from work. Some pious soul is bound to find his widow and insist, "Don't cry, honey. God doesn't make mis-takes." Someone else is going to tell her that God needed him worse than she did. I've wondered many times about what biblical passages they might cite to justify such comments. There seems to be some assumed benefit in excusing the drunken driver and blaming (or crediting) God with the slaughter.

I heard the following comments after several deaths, all within a two-week period:

"Sooner or later God is going to get you."

"God will get you in the end."

"God had numbered his days, and when they ran out, God took him."

"I don't understand why he had to die, but God doesn't make mistakes."

"God must have needed another bud for his rose garden." (Wouldn't it be interesting to hear the biblical proof text for *that* one?)

"You never know when the Lord's gonna snatch you from this old world, do you?"

"God knows best. He won't put more on you than you can bear."

Many seem convinced that God *takes* every life. They leave no room for evil actions of another, for chance, for disease, for personal negligence, for health-destroying behavior, or for anything but the intervening hand of God.

If I sound concerned, it is because I have attempted many times to minister to the problem of rage against God that has surfaced months or years later because of such comments. Many conclude, "If that is the kind of God we have, I want nothing to do with him. Who could love a God like that?" When God is depicted as a big bully who pushes people around to take what he wants, or kills whom he wants, the anger against him is likely to be buried deep within, out of both guilt and fear. Guilt, because we are likely to have been taught that we should never get angry with God. "He always knows best." And we may fear in the presence of such great power. If he brings tragedy into human life on a whim or out of love, just imagine what he might do out of wrath.

For those who may remember the scriptural passage that says "The fear of the Lord is the beginning of wisdom" (Prov. 9:10), remember that the word *fear* also means "profound reverence and awe." I'm saying all of this to remind you of the danger of saying things to people that will kindle anger against God. After all, it's hard to trust one of whom you are terribly frightened, or with whom you are very, very angry. Do we dare presume to declare precisely what God does or does not do in a particular life?

When you speak of God to those in distress, remind them of his love, of his care, of his presence, and compassion. But while they are still on the scene in which they have received the sad news of death, don't expect them to hear a lot of what you have to say in your efforts to help. Their minds are too fogged by the pain of loss.

Let's take it slowly now as we approach that person who has just lost a loved one. What should we *know?* What should we *do?* What should we *say* or refuse to say? And what should we try to *be* to that person? We'll deal with these questions along the way as we try to minister to Helen Jackson.

2

That Crucial First Hour

Let's go back now to the emergency room where Helen, Fred Jackson's widow, is coming through the door. She doesn't even know she's a widow now. All she knows is that Fred has been in an accident. She has had no time to prepare herself. Those who watch a loved one die over a long period of time enter their grief long before the actual death. But this one has been sudden.

That first hour after learning of a loved one's death is one of the most crucial hours of life. How people handle that initial hour of grief will almost certainly influence their spiritual, emotion, and physical well-being for many years to come. Though we will be supportive, a major part of our ministry at this time is to try to help Helen use the experience constructively. You've got to say something. What?

Are you *sure* he is dead? That's always the first question to ask yourself before you tell any loved one of a death. Has he been officially pronounced dead by the doctor? Some people adjust quickly, beginning to cut their ties immediately with their most beloved family members. I have seen people injured for a lifetime by misinformation concerning the death of a loved one. One woman comes to mind who told of hearing that her husband had been killed. She dropped into a chair and began to weep. Less than five minutes later a doctor came out and told her there had been a mistake. Her husband was still alive. He fully recovered within a few weeks. She rejoiced, but many years later she confided, "I loved that man dearly, and still do. But the moment I heard he was gone I cut some sort of tie with him. I was thrilled beyond description that he was still alive, but for some reason I have never understood, I have never felt quite as close to him as I did before." Her experience seems to be representative of many who have been told in error of the death of someone loved.

In the case of Fred Jackson, the nurse has told you clearly that he is dead. It comes from a professional person who has firsthand information. Before I tell a family their loved one is dead, I always want firsthand information if I have any way at all to get it.

For the sake of a point, let's suppose that the doctor had met you and suggested that he, too, wanted to be there when the family is told of the death. That would not be unusual if the patient has died following a period of illness. Be certain who is going to tell the family. Don't confront the family with you and the doctor each expecting the other to do the talking. Agree before you go to the family. Most doctors I've worked with along the way have preferred that I, the minister, do the informing of a death. That probably was not any part of his training. He's no more comfortable with the task than anyone else. In fact, if he feels any sense of failure in not having been able to keep the patient alive, he may be quite uncomfortable. Whatever his choice, it is better not to argue the case if he wants to give the bad news. The doctor is the captain of the medical team. He may, therefore, see anything related to the patient as his responsibility. After he informs the family, you will have your turn. With some exceptions, he'll gladly give it to you. Not many doctors, or anyone else, will debate the role of one who offers a spiritual ministry to those who mourn.

Right now, you are fortunate. You are face-to-face with the person who has to be told of the death. That seems best. If you sometimes have to tell the bad news by phone, try to arrange to have someone with the person you must inform. Even a long-distance call to a neighbor can be helpful. "Mrs. Livingston, your neighbor next door must be told some bad news. Would it be possible for you to go over within the next few minutes to be with her? I will be calling her five minutes from now," would be a typical part of such a conversation. (I have never had a neighbor refuse to cooperate with such a request.) But distance is no problem here. The one to whom you must minister now is right in front of you. How do you tell her?

"Helen, its bad. Let's step into this room" (to some convenient place away from the gazing eyes of the public if possible). Any "beating around the bush" is going to create problems. The anxiety stirred by a lot of preparatory sentences only makes things worse. Don't waste your time trying to find words that will make it easy for her. There are none. Forget the "I'm-sorry-but-I-have-some-bad-news. You-know-that-Fred-sometimes-drives-too-fast-and-when-people-drive-too-fast-they-sometimes-get-terribly-hurt" routine. And I have heard it go on and on. It looks terrible on paper. But it sounds worse to the person who hears it.

There's no easy way! Across the years, I've ministered to at least two thousand families at the time of death. I've long ago concluded that it is a waste of time and effort to try to find easy words to announce that a loved one is dead. (By now, you may be wishing I would go ahead and complete my point.) Make it straight, clear, and simple. "Helen, the accident was terrible. Brace yourself. Fred was killed."

It sounds harsh and cruel. But death *is* often harsh and cruel. When it comes unexpectedly, it is almost always that way. I will patiently listen to any rebuttal with an alternate response. But my own experience and that of others with comparable experience insists that the straightforward, clear pronouncement is ultimately the most merciful approach.

Note that I suggested the most simple, clearly understood language that spoke of "death." This is not the time for vague language that speaks of someone having "gone away," or having "expired," or having "gone to be with the Lord." They truly may have gone to be with the Lord, but this is not the time for those words. This moment calls for the language of death. Use no religious language that would deny the terrible truth, but help them to use their religious resources to face death and to deal constructively with it. For the next few weeks, anything you say about Fred's death should be in the language of death. No matter how devoted a Christian Fred was, as long as his family lives on planet Earth, he is dead to their relationships.

When you've announced his death, the most likely response will be shock, with the outward expression of disbelief. "No!"

Such an effort to deny reality may last for only a moment, but for some people it will continue for *years*. People use denial until they can pull together enough resources to deal more constructively with the loss. It was not the language that induced the shock. It was the truth in what was said. You probably wish you could lessen the pain, but you should say nothing that will support denial. The degree to which one breaks with reality is the degree to which he is psychotic (insane). Your mission here is to help them adjust to reality, not to deny it! It is not necessary to argue. Simply use the language of death when speaking of the death.

When a death is unexpected as was Fred's, the loved ones may have a hard time believing that it has really happened. "No! No! No! I won't believe you!" A few minutes later she may again deny what she has heard. "It can't be true. I just talked with him a while ago. He can't be dead. He's *not* dead." The longer she resists the truth, the more potentially dangerous it is to her mental, physical, and spiritual health. If this kind of denial continues for as long as ten to fifteen minutes, you have one healthy thing to do. And that is going to be terribly painful.

Excuse yourself, and go find the person in charge of the emergency room or who has had the primary responsibility for caring for the patient. You do not have to be demanding, but you must assume the authority you have in the ministering role. Clearly and matter-of-factly declare that it seems necessary for Mrs. Jackson to see her dead husband's body. (In this instance, she has not asked. But with rare exceptions, if the family makes the request, you should attempt to aid in getting that permission.)

Since many emergency room personnel have not been trained in this phase of service, they may seem shocked that you would suggest such a thing. You now must be an educator. State as clearly and as briefly as possible, "Experience insists that when persons are having trouble accepting the reality of a death, seeing the body often helps them to make the adjustment." Only if the face is totally mutilated may this not be best. It sometimes will be necessary to cover parts of the face or head to protect the family from the absolute horror of open wounds. This is the task of the emergency room staff. They may also want to "clean the patient up a little." When permission is granted by the emergency room staff, you will return to Helen.

If she is still refusing to accept that Fred is truly dead, ask as kindly as you know how, "Helen, would you like to see Fred's body?" Across the years, I have never seen a denying person say no.

Having taken the ministering role, it is now your task to go with them. Be prepared for anything at this point. She may faint. It may be your job to try to catch her and help her down easily. Lay her out flat. Spirits of ammonia at her nose will revive her. Time will too. It's just slower. At some point in the process, she may scream. If you knew from prior experience that she was one likely to scream when highly upset, you should have reminded her before going in that she should try to remain quiet if possible, for the sake of other patients.

Don't interfere if she wants to touch him, or even if she wants to kiss him. Your own feelings may tear *you* apart. But this is *her* occasion to do as she feels the need. Ask her, "Helen, if he were alive this moment, has anything been left unsaid that you would like to tell him before you leave?" If you get any impression that she would like to do so, ask her if she would like to be alone with his body for a few minutes.

That time with her dead husband's body can be extremely valuable. She can express love or regret or anything else that she feels. A few moments talking to that dead body may keep her from needing many an hour later in some counselor's office.

When she talked to him before, she has always gotten some response. It was not always good, nor was it always bad, but she did get *some* response. Before, when she has given, she has received *something*. But now she gets *no* response. Relationships grow in an atmosphere of love. They will even continue for many years in an atmosphere of hate. But indifference is the ultimate in rejection. And nothing can be more indifferent than a nongiving, nonresponsive dead body. That silence and unresponsiveness is often felt as a kind of rejection that helps facilitate the breaking of the ties between them. It helps her to let go of the relationship. But the severing of that tie inflicts a gaping wound across the soul.

During the early phase of her grief, not only are her emotions torn, we can expect some physical reactions as well. They usually come early in the grief process and are short-lived, but they may recur again and again.

She may feel an emptiness within her chest, as though something has been literally removed from the region of her heart. The sense of emotional emptiness becomes physical. An aching in the region of the heart has given us the words *heartache* and *heartbreak*.

An aching tightness in the throat—even a choking sensation—is not unusual. The grieving often experience a shortness of breath and frequent need for sighing. Within ten minutes after entering acute grief, Helen may feel so physically depleted she cannot walk. It is a feeling somewhat comparable to having labored without a break for many hours, arriving at a point of physical exhaustion. Though I have helped many people get away from the scene by wheelchair, I must admit that I had to experience a loss within my own family before I could believe the sense of depletion could be so total.

It is obvious that amid such a rapid loss of emotional and physical energy, little that we say or do is going to be of much help. We need then to ask a more serious question of ourselves, "What can I *be* to this person?"

I suspect we are approaching one of the most neglected dimensions of ministry—the ministry of "being." (Throughout the remainder of this chapter, I will italicize the word *be* when I want to call attention to this particular ministry.) Maybe it has been neglected because it sounds somewhat intangible or philosophical. Yet it is far more concrete and common to human experience than it may sound.

The more you watch and listen, the more you will see the *ministry of being* in action. You will see it only where relationships are close and warm. And you will have to listen for what is *not* said and for the subtle inflections in the voice as you hear what *is* said.

Helen has learned that her husband was killed and has begun to collect herself when her best friend, Louise, comes bursting through the door. Watch and listen to what goes on. Louise works in an all-night diner. She is still wearing her waitress's uniform. By the time Helen is to her feet, fresh tears fill her eyes. Louise tosses her purse toward a chair. "Helen, I came just as soon as I heard." The two women stand with their arms around one another. They weep unashamedly together. "I knew you'd come." They move toward chairs, and Helen begins with the details. "Well, like I told you last Sunday, Fred had been talking about having some pains in his chest. He had worked real late and was on his way home. For some peculiar reason he lost control of his car. Maybe he went to sleep at the wheel. We don't know, but I have an idea that . . . ." And five minutes later Helen is still talking, and Louise is giving only an occasional nod of the head and enough inquiry to make it clear she is still interested.

Now let's look at Louise's ministry of being. I could just as easily have used a man or men to illustrate what I'm talking about. Neither men nor women have any special claim to the ministry of being.

Try to *be* there geographically. But circumstances may demand that you *be* there at the end of a telephone. Remember when Louise came in, Helen spoke of being glad her friend had come. She wasn't concerned with what Louise had to say. She needed *her*. Physical presence is preferred, but even being there by phone is better than not being there at all.

Being truly "with" someone requires a harmonious relationship. This requires the participation and efforts on the part of both parties. We never minister, even in a crisis, until we are authorized to do so. I say this to remind you that not every relationship contains a potential for ministry. You will not always minister just because you try to do so. Helen truly "welcomed" Louise into her moments of sorrow.

Louise could only come to Helen geographically. That is, she could only make herself available. Only when Helen came to her was there any possible ministry. This is true no matter what the length of the relationship. Ministers in institutional settings, usually under the title of "Chaplains," visit and minister to total strangers. They can only go to the person geographically; they can only make themselves available. Before they can have a ministry, the person they visit must allow them to do so. They must say, in effect, "I authorize you to *be* my minister."

Of course, this means that we always run the risk of having our ministry rejected. If you are a person who cannot accept at least some sense of rejection, you had better back off. Every person reserves (and deserves) the right to say by word or action or attitude, "No thank you. I do not want what you have to offer." Millions say that to God every day. If they do so to God, we certainly cannot expect them to accept what we have to offer as his servants.

Remember that Louise came "bursting through the door." She had not even taken the time to change dresses. It appeared that she had dropped what she was doing to be with her friend Helen. This is a part of the ministry of being. Not only was Louise willing to *be* there, she seemed *eager* to do so. *Be* eager to become involved in the lives of others. If for some reason you cannot do so with this person, try to get someone who can.

We represent not only ourselves, but the community of mankind. And, more specifically, we represent the caring community of Christ's church and Jesus Christ himself. We symbolically represent God's presence and help amid life's painful loss. But carefully examine your motives. *Be* watchful of yourself. You just may be more concerned with fulfilling a need within yourself than within another. Work out your own needs at another time and another place. Helen needs the best of you and her friend right now. The two women embraced as they met. We may be afraid to openly put our arms around someone, even someone in the depths of despair. Our culture is so deeply infected with sexual misbehavior and suspicion we become more and more afraid of the physical touch. Shall I touch or refuse to touch? Will I be accused of trying to become too familiar—or seductive—or homosexual?

Most people need to be touched far more than they are, but a part of our cultural sickness seems to force us to link the touch with sexual misconduct. Yes, we have to *be* discrete, but when all the warnings have been sounded, we have to recognize that the human touch has a strange power for imparting strength that no one yet has been fully able to comprehend.

What is it within a firm hand on the shoulder of one in fear or sorrow? It gives strength. Why? How? What is that power in the lingering handshake at the bedside of one who knows he is dying? Almost anyone who has been really down and has felt the touch of a concerned friend knows exactly what I'm talking about. It has similarities to that which many have received during the "laying on of hands" in an ordination service.

I have yet to talk with anyone who could fully explain that

experience. What is there? A power is imparted. People feel energized. Something flows from one person to another. Jesus was so sensitive to this that when a woman touched merely the hem of his garment, he felt something of himself go out to her. It was healing. And something healing is in the touch of a caring person to one in distress! I suspect the early church was more aware of this power than is modern man. Remember that the "laying on of hands" held a significant place in the *healing* ministry of the early church.

Is it possible that, with some exceptions, we moderns generally have let go unnoticed a vast reserve of power comparable to an undiscovered oil reserve only a few feet below the surface? When the oil is pumped to the surface, it may be used to fuel an ambulance or a bomber. The human touch may be used to heal or to ignite passions. Those who would minister with the touch carry also the responsibility to *be* discrete and to *be* aware of their own motivations and needs. But we must also *be* alert to read the response and even to anticipate the response of the one whom we would touch. Yes, it is complex, and it is potentially dangerous. Maybe that is why it is so neglected.

Before we get too far from Louise and Helen, recall that Louise was a ready listener. Few things are more important for ministering in the wake of death.

Be a listener who will give attention to every detail of a story without interruption. Ask only enough to keep the person talking. Find some good books on counseling, listening, and interviewing techniques. The more you improve your listening skills, the richer your potential for ministry to those in distress. This is too broad a subject to try to develop here, but I'll give some suggested readings in the bibliography at the end of the book.

You learn a lot in the course of listening to the heartaches of people around you. That means that this ministry of listening carries with it a heavy responsibility. It is the responsibility to *be* silent about what you hear. Defenses are often quite low amid fear and pain and sorrow. People often say things they might never otherwise reveal. *Be* worthy of the confidence placed in you.

Confidence in you can lead to confidence placed in God. *Be* courageous enough to represent the Lord whom you serve. If your own experience has been that God walks with those who suffer, tell them. This is *not* the time to tell of your own experience. But it is the time to tell of what you know of God. Have you learned that God will walk *every* step of the way with those who hurt? Then tell them that he will. Have you learned that God imparts strength to endure? Then reassure that he will.

People often feel they will never be able to get through the days ahead. Have you learned that God supplies the needs of today, and that no reserve can be stored for tomorrow? Have you learned God will supply tomorrow's needs as he has supplied the needs of today? Then tell them! Read the sixteenth chapter of Exodus. You will note that manna held in reserve usually spoiled. God seems to have been trying to teach that he would provide for them as their needs arose—day by day.

Be confident in the power of God. Faith is contagious. Your own faith in God and your faith in the person to whom you minister tends to be catching. That means you will *be* prayerful. Talk to God. Take your concerns for Helen before our Lord, but not necessarily at this moment, and not necessarily while you are in her presence. Some people will not yet be in the state of mind for it. Bear one another's burdens. And bear a concern for her and her children, knowing that, with the help of people who care and the help of God, she probably will be all right.

Be confident in people and in their ability to adapt. People are not as easily crushed by their painful experiences as we or they may think. They often hit bottom quite hard—but they bounce—maybe not so high sometimes, but far from shattered and still functioning productively. Your own unspoken faith in their ability to survive often goes a long way. However, your "Oh, don't worry. You are going to be all right" may sound so unrealistic that they feel more hopeless than if you said nothing. Some things are best communciated silently as people unconsciously read our attitude toward them. Combine your faith, hope, and love and give it to people. In the language of what I have been calling the ministry of being, *be* loving and expectant as you hold on to hope for their recovery.

No matter how much unspoken hope we hold for the future, we must minister to them in their "now." We still can learn from Helen's friend.

Remember that when Helen saw Louise enter the room, she began to cry. Only a few persons ever seem to accept us with whatever feelings come to the surface. Helen knew immediately that Louise could accept her tears. Many are afraid they will place too heavy a burden on you if they cry with you. *Be* accepting of people's feelings, without rejection or criticism. This time it was sadness and fear. The next time it may be anger or guilt.

Some would criticize Louise for crying with her hurting friend. They insist that when Helen sees Louise's tears she will feel bad (guilty) for causing her friend to suffer too. Maybe. But an equally strong argument holds that Helen will be helped by seeing that her friend cared so deeply that she would be moved to tears. Both are probably valid arguments at times. You will try, then, to *be* sensitive to what seems best under the existing circumstances. Somebody might consider you wrong or inappropriate in whichever you do. *Be* willing to risk making a mistake. Even if you are in error, they probably will recognize later that you cared enough to try. That's more than most will do.

Our culture places an additional burden on the grieving. It's a "no win" bind—a cultural conflict. On one side cultural pressure says, "Your tears show that you are weak." From the other side comes the pressure that says, "Your lack of tears shows that you didn't care." The truth is that most people need to cry more than they permit themselves.

When persons begin to cry, we want to *be* observant of *how* they cry. On some occasions, when people are highly upset, they will cry in a shallow, short-breathed pant. This can quickly lead to an oxygen-carbon dioxide imbalance in the blood, known as hyperventilation. The hands and feet may tingle, and their lips may feel numb. Crying persons tend to feel weak. They may, at that time, respond to authority when they might otherwise refuse. The person showing symptoms of hyperventilation needs your help. With slow deliberate speech, firmly instruct, "Close your mouth and breathe through your nose. Breathe deeply, but slowly." You may want to warn that their breathing pattern can make them nauseous. And if they continue, they will pass out.

A simple first-aid technique suggests you place a paper bag over their nose and mouth while they breathe several times. Breathing their own expelled air quickly restores the proper balance in the bloodstream, restoring them to consciousness. As they recover from this kind of faint, a mild convulsion and nausea are common.

But no matter how they do it, PEOPLE NEED TO CRY. If you get the feeling they want to do so, use the words that offer permission. Not only do they fear criticism for weakness if they cry, they also are concerned for *you*. They know you may feel something of their pain. Your permission says, in effect, "I am willing to endure whatever the sight of your tears stirs within me." I wonder if accepting this sort of voluntary load is what Jesus had in mind when he taught, "Deny yourself and take up your cross and follow me" (see Matt. 16:24). If you have the impression that tears are near the surface but are being held back for any reason, say it clearly, "It's all right to cry. Let it come out."

Just as the pressure cooker for the kitchen stove is made with a relief valve, God has made members of the human race with a relief valve for the lessening of inner pressures from life's hurts. Just as tears wash impurities from the eyes, they also help wash hurt from the soul.

I hear it suggested from time to time that the Christian is not

to grieve because of a biblical injunction that says the Christian
need not sorrow "as others which have no hope" (1 Thess.
4:13). But Christians do, indeed, sorrow amid their sense of
grief. They may feel a quiet sense of satisfaction in the assur-
ance that the loved one is safe in the arms of our Lord. But at
the same moment they may feel *an even* greater loss than the
non-Christian.

I am convinced that Christians, in general, tend to build
deeper relationships than non-Christians. They have a greater
sense of commitment, and have usually given more of themselves to the love relationship. Having *mutually* invested more
into the relationship, the personal loss is greater when their
loved one dies. It is, therefore, quite appropriate and healthy
for the Christian to weep at the time of a great loss. Even
Jesus wept on a similar occasion (John 11:35).

You will not only permit tears, you will encourage them!
This is best done by getting the person to talk about the loved
one. Encourage the grieving one to remember, to talk about
"old times." Encourage the survivor who begins to talk about
the kind of person the deceased was.

Expect glorification of the dead at this point. Don't try to
force the survivors to face the negative parts of the relationship
or of the personality. It may be months before they can permit
themselves to look at that. They've already got about all they
can handle.

They have lost a part of their life's emotional structure. A
member of their family of relationships has been cut off—an
amputation without the benefit of anesthesia. They are emotionally crippled—handicapped—temporarily or permanently.
And nothing you can say or do is going to stop the pain.

But when the emotions are raw—when the nerve endings
of the soul are exposed, people are in touch with feelings and
attitudes of those around them. They grasp your love and
compassion.

But they rarely grasp much of what you say. Maybe at least

some small portion is absorbed into the soul where it promotes healing. Recall the last time you were hurt deeply from a great loss. If you have had none, ask someone who has. Kind words, lines of great and comforting poetry, or even passages of Scripture are lost amid the pain. People simply do not remember them. For some reason that I do not fully understand, the most positive of our words are not remembered.

Maybe they are rejected partly because kind words suggest that we think we understand. People amid great pain are often convinced that *no one* can possibly understand. And maybe they are right.

This is not the time to try to prove we understand by sharing our own painful experience that seems somewhat comparable to the one they currently endure. Friends often insist, "I know just how you feel. Last year when my husband died I just knew I'd die too, etc., etc." But every relationship is unique. Much of the pain comes from memories of those events that created that relationship. Even the memories of identical twins will be different. They each have unique joys and laughters, angers and regrets, and all the rest that make every relationship and its set of memories entirely different from those of any other person on Earth. And when a loved one has died, the whole past that related to that person seems to flood the mind. It is highly presumptuous to assume that we really fully comprehend what they are going through. We don't. Yes, our own loss gets us vaguely close to it but not close enough to understand totally. "I know just how you feel" may be well-meaning, but the words usually sound phony to the one in pain.

In addition, any efforts to prove our point by the sharing of our own loss experience tends to weigh them down even more. This is their time. The writer of Ecclesiastes suggested there is a time for just about everything. This is *their* time to grieve. Your sharing of your similar loss tends to make them feel robbed. You've already had your time. You should have already dealt with your own griefs. If you have not done so, find someone who is not already feeling some fresh loss with whom you can share yours. Each person with whom we share it takes on some of that pain. Acutely grieving persons have about all they feel they can endure for the time being. Don't give them more by handing them yours.

For each person who is likely to add to the hurt, someone else is going to try to take all the hurt away—with drugs. My limited perspective sometimes gives me the impression·that at least half of the adult population is carrying private supplies of sedatives. And they are all too eager to share them at the first sight of a tear. When the grieving person first reaches for a handkerchief, others start reaching for their purses and pill-boxes. If friends or relatives don't offer it, some equally well-meaning doctor or nurse just may. I have helped carry people who were so heavily sedated at the time of grief they could not walk.

Many physicians have little more special training in dealing with people who are emotionally distressed by grief than any other typical college graduate. A study reported by *Newsweek* magazine revealed that only 7 of 107 US medical schools taught a full-term course dealing with death and bereavement.[1] (My broad acquaintance with ministers makes me suspect that a comparable survey of theological schools would show a similar lack in theological education.) That means that having read this far into this book, you have more specific instruction in helping people cope with painful loss than a large percentage of highly trained persons whose place of service requires them to work with the bereaved. Most doctors and nurses (and ministers) have gone into their fields of service because they truly want to relieve human suffering. In an emotional crisis, they easily forget the difference between physical suffering and emotional suffering. They don't intend to harm. They *want* to help.

Sedation at the time of loss accomplishes at least one thing. It stops the emotional outflow long enough to get the grieving out of sight.

Virtually all efforts to stop the grieving from expressing their tears is hypocritical. It is always piously done under the guise of trying to stop them for their own good. We tend to believe something terrible will happen if people become hysterical. Having worked with at least two thousand families at the time of death, I've seen some pretty upset people—many I suppose, would have been called hysterical. So what?! The most *violently* upset person I remember was as calm as a kitten within ten minutes or less. In more than twenty-one years of hospital ministry, I have yet to see one person who seemed harmed by the most extreme outburst.

On the other hand, almost any minister or other counselor you talk with can tell you of person after person who has been injured by their *lack* of emotional outlet following the loss of a loved one! I have counseled with people whose emotional knots and kinks have become more and more tightly bound for periods ranging to almost forty years! Time and again, the evidence insists that for some reason, they were not able to express themselves adequately at the time of their loss.

Timing is important. The sooner the better. Any blockage has the danger of becoming a permanent blockage.

When others are not trying to stop people from crying, they are trying to stop themselves. The release of tears is thought to be a show of weakness. Men especially have a hard time here. Many have heard all their lives, *"Men* don't cry." Masculinity is at stake. One man said it classically, "I'm afraid that if I cry I will turn into a woman." People who are emotionally, physically, and spiritually healthy *do* cry at the appropriate time. And the loss of a loved one is an appropriate time. *Any man who loses his masculinity with a few tears has had little masculinity to lose!* He will not have lost much. The man who has the keys to his identity locked up in his tear glands is in deep trouble! Tears are neither masculine or feminine. They are human.

People often feel they have to restrain tears for the sake of other family members. "I've got to hold up for Mama." If the children step out of the room, Mama is likely to say, "I've got to hold up for the sake of the children." Everybody is often try-

ing to hold up for the sake of trying to support everybody else
as though God were too weak to support the whole family at
one time. Many people feel they are expected to demonstrate
their Christian faith by refusing to cry. How many times have I
seen someone look up quickly trying to wipe away all tears,
"Oh, I'm sorry, Reverend. I ought not to cry like this. I ought
to have more faith." Is the show of tears really a denial of
faith? Or is it possible for tears to be a *proclamation* of faith?" Is
it not possible for one to say, in effect, "I am weak at this time.
I do not have to pretend to be strong. I do not have to find
strength within myself. My God will sustain me through this
time of personal weakness. I may cry. I may scream. I may lie
on the floor, emotionally and physically depleted, with the full
confidence that my Lord Jesus will walk with me through this
dark, sad valley in the very shadow of death." To those of
faith, *do not hesitate to give reassurance.* People often need
to be reminded of God's understanding, of the appropriate-
ness of their tears, and of God's availability as a source of
strength.

People are in a receptive stance when personal weakness is
admitted. As long as one finds adequate strength in himself,
he does not even recognize the need for strength from God.
Many are so proud they find it hard to accept a gift from God
even when they do recognize the need. Many see themselves
as too unworthy for God to be interested in them.

If you have any faith—if you have any sense of commis-
sion, this is the time to speak boldly as a prophet for God.
"God will not leave you nor forsake you. Take refuge in the
arms of God. *God is* your refuge." Keep yourself out of the
conversation. Use no phrases such as "I think . . ." or "I believe . . . ." Proclamation weakens with any personal opinion.
Your authority is God's written word. Speak "Thus saith the
Lord . . ."; "God says. . . ." If you are aware of the Scriptures, you know that God is interested in *all* that people experience. In the midst of loss, all is not sorrow.

Most persons who recently have lost a loved one are feeling

some degree of anger. It is stirred by the sense of helplessness and the frustration of being unable to do anything to change it. Death reminds us that we are not in complete control. The anger is often free-floating—pointed at nothing in particular and at everything and everyone in general. And don't be surprised if some are angry even with God. Most who even barely believe a God exists are convinced that he is ultimately responsible by directly causing or passively permitting all tragedy. (And be alert to how often those who deny God exists do so in rejection because they are angry with him.) Anger against God is among the most common of grief reactions.

And guess who is likely to catch the full brunt of the rage? The pastor or the lay minister or anyone who represents God is likely to be the target. Many a pastor has packed his bags and moved on, crying within himself, "But what did I do wrong? The very people I gave the most of myself to have run me off."

The religious worker is the nearest and most available target. He is truly seen as God's ambassador. In the time of hostilities, the ambassador of any land is the first to feel any attack. We like to think that people are drawn to God by their troubles. But if they believe God is the cause of their troubles they may go the other way. Note how many people leave the church within six months after a death in the family!

What do you do with this kind of problem? *Hear it out!* Give people a chance to put their anger into words. They may be somewhat surprised and relieved when God fails to strike them dead with a bolt of lightning.

Few people change their theological position during the throes of the crisis of grief. If you want to help them with such theological issues, do it before the crisis or in the months after it, but don't expect to be heard during the time of most intense pain. This is the time for listening. This is the time for reassuring that they are still loved in spite of their rage. When people feel that God either has turned his back on them or has placed a heavy hand of chastisement upon them, they often feel totally cursed. Any condemnation from you for their anger will leave them feeling "doubly damned."

God is not the only one with whom people get angry at the time of grief. Family members who have been less than perfect may catch some of it too. Others get angry with those who do not share a loss comparable to their own. Doctors and nurses are common targets. You serve a great need when you simply sit and listen. You do not have to agree with them! Neither do you have to defend them. Just give them the privilege of "letting off steam."

People often get angry with hospitals. Someone has suggested that most hospital chaplains annually save their institutions an amount equal to several times their salary. They do so by giving people an opportunity to vent their rage before they have a chance to file a legal suit.

Most people probably would be surprised to know how many get angry with the dead for dying. It is often associated with a feeling of abandonment. Helen might easily feel, "Fred left me at a time when I needed him to help rear our three children." Or the feelings of anger may grow out of the feelings related to the work or the problems created by the death. "How dare him to walk off and die, leaving me with all of his affairs to put in order!" Helen must decide, "Should I sell his expensive tools or try to determine where to store them for fifteen years until little Danny is old enough to use them?" No matter how he died, the frustration and anger might have been stirred. But deep within, a voice may seem to say, "You should never feel angry with the dead. He didn't die on purpose. And you ought not get angry with someone who cannot defend himself." That seems immoral to most, which leaves them feeling guilty. That guilt can easily ignite anger against oneself. Any time we fail to do or to think or to feel as we have told ourselves we ought, we usually will feel guilty, and then angry with ourselves. That means that guilt with its associated anger is one of the most common factors in all of man's grief.

People remember their deeds and their misdeeds; what they said and what they ought to have said; what they were and what they should have been. But who has taken advantage of every opportunity to express love that life has provided? This is said only to remind us that we have no room to be judgmental. Do not seek to justify their behavior. Leave justification to God. *Sin you justify will be sin for which people will not seek forgiveness. The excuse you offer cuts them off from the grace God offers!*

When people are talking about their regrets, they are confessing. They are following biblical teaching: "Confess your faults one to another, and pray for one another, that ye may be healed" (Jas. 5:16). And anyone who ministers in the name of Jesus Christ and hears confession must hear it with reverence. When you hear confession, you are on holy ground. Take off your shoes. You are being permitted into the place where normally only God is occasionally allowed. That means you will be prayerful as you listen. That person may appear to be looking at you, but he may be seeing beyond you straight into the face of God. Tell of his love. Remind of his willingness to forgive.

Reassure that *all said is in confidence.* If you have not done so, you will do well, right now, to take a vow of silence: "As a Christian, serving in the name of Jesus Christ, I will divulge no personal or family matters committed to my keeping in the practice of my ministry." Physicians and nurses are required to take a similar vow. Why should it not be required of one serving in a Christian ministry? Many people are terrified of the idea of admitting fault to another for fear of being quoted all over the community. They have heard it! The day you said yes to any Christian ministry was the day you forfeited the luxury (and sin) of gossip—about *anybody!*

If you cannot, with the help of God, keep confidences, resign your position now, before you do more harm than good!

During those days when grief is fresh, when all emotions are raw, people often divulge family matters never otherwise exposed. Defenses are down. People are vulnerable. Even if nothing is said directly, you get a view of family relationships in a perspective never otherwise seen. You hear by suggestion and inuendo. You pick up facial expressions and glances across the room among family members. Wounds that are decades old are often laid bare. Old family feuds suddenly erupt, and sharp words are exchanged.

Other embarrassed family members may glance uneasily toward you and want to scream to their own, "Shut up! Do you want the family dirty linen laid out before the whole world!" It could easily have arisen too quickly for you to have been able to excuse yourself in advance. You may leave with a simple comment that every family has matters that are purely private *and need to stay that way.* And when you have gone, you will never repeat what you have seen or heard. That will be just one more secret you will carry.

Rarely are all the feelings experienced at the time of a death related to the current loss. We each have what some have called a "grief compartment"—a little storage place within our personalities reserved for the feelings and memories related to our losses. Problems arise when we open the compartment to place the fresh loss inside. The most painful ones will usually have worked their way to the top.

This means that *new grief is almost always mixed with old grief,* but rarely do people admit it. For instance, if Mama has died ten years ago, people seem to feel there should be no remaining pain—as though there were something mentally sick about it. Therefore, when Papa dies, children will secretly reach into the "grief compartment" and take out their unresolved grief for Mama and work on it too. But they may also use the occasion to pull out several other unresolved griefs and secretly deal with them also.

This is one reason people often seem to grieve much at the time of the death of someone with whom they were not even close. People will rarely discuss these other losses freely unless you give them clear permission. Listen for their references to prior losses. For instance, if someone says something similar to, "Papa's been gone for ten years, and now it's Mama," respond with something comparable to: "It sounds as though your mother's death stirs fresh feelings around your father's death." Then listen!

And remind members of a family that they need to listen to one another. Remind them of the need to give one another the privilege of talking and of crying with one another. They may need to hear that the granting of permission to talk, and to cry, and to laugh, may be one of the best ways they can express love for one another in the days and weeks ahead.

This may be as good a place as any to remind you that people often need permission to laugh during their time of grief as much as they need permission to cry. They are sometimes afraid their behavior will be seen as inappropriate, or uncaring, if they permit themselves to laugh during their time of grief. When you boil it down, I am really suggesting that people should be permitted to be themselves—not controlled or manipulated into acting in *any* way that we or others think they *ought* to act. This is true either in that first hour after the death or in the months that follow.

But we are not even away from the death scene yet, and practical matters still may need to be handled. Do family members need to be called? Local or distant? The local Red Cross office still seems to be the most direct way of getting in touch with military personnel for emergency leaves. You can often help the family by offering to make the calls for them. Some will be so upset they cannot remember the phone number they have called daily for many years. Some will prefer to busy themselves by personally making the calls. That is their privilege. You are there to help, not to force yourself on anyone.

Does anything need to be taken care of before they go home? The hospital probably will not want to bother the family with financial matters right after the death. (That is one of the reasons hospitals commonly lose, in bad debts, as much as a thousand dollars per day for each hundred patients they serve.) We can assume Helen will take care of the bill in the next few days after the funeral.

Does the hospital have forms to sign related to the dead patient? Probably there is at least one—the form releasing the body to a specific mortuary. The suspected cause of the patient's death, the attending physician's interests, hospital policy, and individual state laws will determine if a request is made for an autopsy. Beware of giving advice!

Once, in a space of two minutes, I watched a pastor cost a family ten thousand dollars, encourage a decision that divided a family, and cause indescribable emotional conflict that injured a whole church. The incident was similar to Fred's. A man was nearing home, having spent many hours on the road, when his car gradually left the road, rolled a couple of times, and came to rest on its wheels. He died the next day, apparently of a blood clot on the brain. The attending physician suggested an autopsy, and the family was ready to sign the proper forms giving permission, when the pastor objected saying that he did not think it the "right thing to do." The man had gone to sleep at the wheel and had died as the result of the accident. It was clear and simple.

But weeks later, the insurance company did not see it quite the same way. They were not about to pay on a double indemnity claim for death by accident. They agreed that the accident *might* have caused the blood clot that killed the victim, but they insisted that according to the evidence, it was just as likely that the victim, while driving, had formed a blood clot that had gone to the brain, and this had caused the accident! No one disagreed that the patient had died of a blood clot on the brain—but did the accident cause the blood clot, or did the blood clot cause the accident? Only an autopsy would have determined which had caused the other. The last I heard, the family was still arguing among themselves about digging up the body, and the pastor had hurriedly left town amid an uproar in the church. That is not quite in keeping with a ministry of reconciliation.

I know of no modern biblical interpretation that would seem to be against the postmortem examination (autopsy). I recognize, however, that some believers would quickly point to a passage they interpret as being against the practice. After all, it was this issue that held back study of the human anatomy for several centuries. It was largely this issue that first separated the physician from the clergy. The church of that day was *violently* against internal study of anatomy.

Modern objection to the autopsy is almost purely based on emotional sensitivities. "I just can't bear the idea of them cutting on him after he is dead," or, "I'm afraid we'll be able to see the evidence when he is in the casket" are the frequent types of comments. Pathologists (medical doctors who actually perform the autopsy) insist they can do the work, leaving nothing to be seen by those who view the body in the casket.

Since laws are rigid and penalties severe for performing an autopsy without adequate permission, only the family or court appointed officials can authorize the autopsy. All states with which I am familiar require two witnesses *to the signing* of the permission forms. You may help by signing as a witness if you are asked to do so by the hospital authority. If it seems crude or even cruel to ask for such a painful decision at this time, remember there is no other time to ask it.

It has been a trying experience. As little as five minutes and as much as two hours may have passed. The family (and you) may be thoroughly emotionally drained. Many find prayer a time for recharging that which seems emotionally and spiritually depleted. No matter how much *you* may feel the need, or how prayerful the family normally is, offer an option. If you say, "Helen, let's pray before we go," or, "Would you like me to offer prayer before we go," she or few other persons have the courage to say, "No, I'm really not in the frame of mind or spirit right now." Though it might be far beyond your understanding, she may have any number of private reasons for not wanting it now. *Provide an option.* "Helen, would you like for me to lead in prayer before you go home, or would you prefer that, instead, I remember you and your family in my private prayers?" The first time someone says, "Thank you. Would you please just remember us as you pray later," you will be glad you offered the option.

Prayer will include thanksgiving for God's love and care for her and her family. Ask that God will help her to endure the loss, that she will be able to find strength and courage in her friends and other members of the family as well as in the fellowship of the church. If you ask God to "Be with her," you may cause her to reflect and wonder how far away he otherwise would be from her. It would not be unusual for her to feel forsaken already. Instead, ask God to remind her of his presence with her and her family, especially during the days and weeks ahead.

One last word before we leave the hospital scene. Does the family need help getting personal belongings to their car? And do they know their way out of the hospital? The many corridors and the sameness of the "landmarks" make most hospitals confusing places for people in a normal state of mind. They seem far worse for those who are emotionally upset.

The nurse will contact the mortuary to request that they pick up the body, but the family will need to call or visit the mortuary to begin initial plans. The mortician will need information for the obituary column of the local newspapers as quickly as possible.

Does Helen need you to go home with her to tell the children what has happened?

If for any reason you feel you should go to her home, discretion would suggest it wise to call and ask your wife or friend to come to the Jackson's home as soon as possible. I dislike sounding crude, but I must deal with issues. Leave no room for suspicion. Protect both your reputation and hers.

3

What Are We Going to Tell the Children?

Whether that trip is one mile or twenty, you will probably wish it were a little longer. You may not talk much. You want time to think. You dread the children's reaction to the loss of their father. They are going to hurt. And we would rather not see that. It is easy, therefore, to fool ourselves and persuade ourselves that our failure to tell children of the death of a parent is purely to protect the children. Indeed, we do wish we could protect children from some of the horrible truths of life. According to statistics, they will have to endure the loss of a loved one on an average of once every six years. The Jackson children have to begin dealing with their first one now. They have to know the truth.

And the same thing would hold for the death of a grandparent or brother or sister or any other person emotionally close to the children. "But can't they be spared such pain of loss?" No! Even the youngest child is better equipped to deal with the truth than he is to deal with deception. Children are sensitive to the emotional state of those around them—especially their parents. They know, "Something's wrong with Mama. What? Have I done something terrible?" They get a glimpse of an occasional tear. They hear the hushed tones of conversation. They have watched families break apart in divorce. "Where's Daddy? Has he left us?" They need the reassurance that those who remain are being truthful with them. They need honesty, even though it is painful for them and for us. Without it, barriers are created, and the child is left to struggle alone with his frightening experience.

Most children have at least some acquaintance with death. They have seen dead insects. A goldfish has died. A family pet has been killed by a car. Or they have seen a dead animal along the roadway. But this is the death of a person—somebody close to them. It is a personal loss. Without plunging into the depths of psychological entanglements, I hope it will suffice to say that children tend to think magically—that somehow their angers or fleeting thoughts can bring things to reality. They can easily conclude that they are responsible for the death or disappearance of the loved one. This tendency will be even stronger if, in a moment of desperation, the parent has screamed, "You'll be the death of me yet. You are driving me crazy." The child, as much as any other person, needs to be permitted, even encouraged, to think aloud and express feelings about the death of one who has been loved. He has lost a source of love. He faces a monumental task of adaptation.

Erna Furman, in her thorough studies of children in grief, reports that children seem to develop the capacity for longing by the end of their first year of life.[1] She also stresses the importance of someone being available to aid the child in the expression of that longing. Neither a surviving parent nor a parent substitute can spare the child the pain and distress of mourning. Their love, however, can help the child to bear it.[2] If the child is not given the opportunity to adequately express his grief, we can expect angers, guilts, prolonged bouts with depression, and even delinquency or physical illness.

When the death has been sudden and the child has no direct involvement, as in the case of Fred Jackson, Erna Furman further reports that the child is helped most when the surviving parent can be the one to broach the news right away.

> A brief preliminary remark helps the child to brace himself a little. "I have something very sad to tell you." . . .

> Sometimes all the details are not even known at first.
> Children seem to feel better when the parent tells them
> that he does not know all the circumstances and will
> share them as he learns about them, than when he delays
> all information until he knows the full story.[3]

The child often wonders, "What is going to happen now?" He
needs reassurance from the surviving parent that the family
will remain together and that his needs will be met in the best
way possible.

It is not yet dawn as you pull into the Jackson's driveway.
The headlights sweep across the yard, and you glimpse the
broken tricycle on the walkway. You remember that the little
one can't be more than three. Helen's voice breaks the silence. "Fred's been working so late. He was going to try to find
time to fix Danny's tricycle next Saturday." Before the engine
dies, the three youngsters are beside the car waiting for the
doors to open. You are glad to see the neighbors who have
come to wait with the children. Amid the jumble of inquiring
voices one says clearly, "Is Daddy all right?" You are aware
that Helen is crying and that the lump in your own throat is so
big you can barely speak. You hear your own voice say, "No.
Let's go on inside, and we'll talk about it." You pretend not to
hear the barrage of questions, but you speak again. "Just another few steps inside and we'll talk about it." On the porch
you realize you are avoiding looking into any of their eyes.
Children are so perceptive, you know they will read the truth if
they get a chance to look you straight in the face. Helen opens
her mouth to speak the terrible news but breaks into uncon-
trolled sobs. You know you've got to be the one to say it. You
perch on the edge of the sofa, and the words come out.
"Children, I have some very bad news for you. Your Daddy
didn't make it. He was dead by the time they got him to the
hospital." The older two scream. Little Danny looks bewil-
dered and moves closer to his mother. It may be days or

weeks before he will really grasp that Daddy won't be home with him again. You wish you were somewhere else—*anywhere* else.

Whether you can put your arms around them while they cry will be determined by a combination of factors in your own personality and in theirs. Do so only if you have the impression they are comfortable with it. If you have the feelings they want to cry, reassure them that it is all right.

They will have questions. Whatever you say must be the truth, though you may not always tell them all the truth you know. For instance, in another situation you would not volunteer that a father was drunk and had killed another person. When they ask about his injuries, you will not go into detail about the gaping bloody hole in his chest made by the steering wheel. You will simply tell them that he had a bad chest injury. While you are with them at this time, and later, there are some things that should and should not be said.

Remind them that death is a natural event. It is the end of every natural life on earth. For their father, it was the natural outcome of the injuries to his body. With such injuries (or sickness, as the case in which we are ministering often will be), the body could not continue to function. You will not say that God took him, or that God must have needed him more than they did (as I have heard on numerous occasions). The child (and many adults) hears such statements as proclaiming God to be a selfish bully who takes what he wants, no matter whom he hurts.

Since Fred Jackson was an active professing Christian, use language that affirms faith in a God who will continue to love them and their father. Say that *after their father died* (that phrase is important), then, God took him home to heaven.

Help the child to understand that the sorrow he sees among the adults is not for their father's current welfare (who may indeed be in a better place). The sorrow is for their own sense of loss of someone who has been special to them. We thus teach the child that it is not death we fear, but it is our own loss of important relationships that causes us to mourn. (Anyone who has been around intense, prolonged suffering has recognized that death can be a true friend.)

I must return to the special emphasis I gave to God having taken him *after he died.* NEVER, in the presence of the child, make reference to the dead as having "gone away" or having "gone to be with the Lord." Children take the words of the adult for exactly what they say. The Jackson children would hear you saying, "Daddy did not want to stay with us. He chose to be with someone else." *That* spells rejection! It creates rage and offers no place to lay it. And many feel they should *never* feel angry with the dead. Such anger and guilt will be turned into added depression or possibly into criminal behavior. Such energy will be channeled, but rarely is it turned in a healthy direction. It is almost always used destructively.

Let's add some other things *not* to say to the child in bereavement. Do not refer to the dead as having "gone to sleep." Many who study human development are convinced that the small child's fight to keep from going to sleep is his fear of not awakening. We'll leave that for professional debate. But there is no serious debate among those who have done counseling that the child takes adult words literally. He may conclude, "Daddy went to sleep, and they put him in a hole in the ground and covered him up. *If I go to sleep the same thing might happen to me."* The father has died, or he was *killed.* That is the truth, and it is the language to use with the children as well as with the adults. Pastors sometimes complain, "But my people don't like for me to use such plain language in the presence of the children." Then it becomes a *pastoral responsibility* to teach the value of plain language and of the dangers of some of the language that tries to skirt reality. Do it before tragedy comes.

Children sometimes have a terrible load placed on them at the death of a parent—especially the parent of the same sex. Wanting to give the child a feeling of importance, someone is likely to say to the little boy whose father has just been killed, as was Fred Jackson, "Son, your daddy is gone. You are going to have to take good care of your mommy and help her a lot." If a little girl's mother has died, she will probably hear something comparable. "Honey, your daddy will need a lot of help now. You will have to be the little woman of the house." Such words should *never* come from the minister.

Imagine the terror the child must feel. Remember—children tend to take words of adults to mean *exactly what they say.* The little boy suddenly sees himself as the primary bread-winner for the family with all the load of responsibility he has recognized that his daddy had carried. The little girl may see herself with the responsibility for preparing the meals and maintaining the household. If the child has known what goes on in the bedroom, he or she may easily assume that sexual relations are included with the responsibility for becoming the little man or little woman of the house. Having counseled for more than twenty years, I have listened many times to the anger, guilt, and fear growing out of the weighty responsibilities laid on the child at the death of the parent. Of course, if the child is permitted, even encouraged, to freely express himself, such issues may be revealed for clarification.

From the moment of death through the day of the funeral is a harried time for most families. The children's concerns and interests ought to be included all the way through. They often feel deprived, even insulted, by being excluded. They need to know what is going on and they need to be a part of it.

> Sometimes families wish to spare the child the anguish of the concrete aspects of the funeral and burial and to spare themselves the additional burden of caring for the child and dealing with his reactions at that time. In some cases this works out well, especially when the child is very young and can remain at home with a trusted adult who can help him with his questions and feelings. When this arrangement is made for older children, they feel left out, deprived of the opportunity to share their feelings with the family and to understand what happened to the body of the dead parent.[4]

Erna Furman's studies clearly indicate the need for the surviving parent to continue the parenting role even amid the stress of dealing with his/her own loss.

But most of us are accustomed to ministering amid something less than the ideal. While we may not "parent" the child, in addition to our prayers, we can offer warmth, encouragement, and a listening ear. Our ministering role requires that we listen as attentively to the child in grief as we do to the adult.

You may say you are not a counselor. That's not what I'm calling for. Only a small percentage of those who read these lines are or ever will be "professional" counselors. If you have a compassionate heart, a listening ear, and the desire to communicate the love of God, you have a lot going for your ministry that many professional counselors don't have. When hearts are broken, people aren't looking for a degree. They are looking for a warm, caring person. We don't earn that. It is what we struggle to become!

Though you may have led in prayer before the family left the hospital, you will again suggest prayer with the option mentioned near the end of chapter 2. You will walk away, leaving them in the care of God and their friends.

If you cannot now do so, ask God to help you to learn to do that. Only *God* can bear all people's burdens—all at one time—and remain healthy. You will do *no one* a service by carrying the burden for Helen's family as you go about the rest of your work. Those who are close to people's hurts may be close to twenty to thirty or more families where there is pain and conflict. Learn to carry one at a time *only while you are with those hurting people* or you endanger yourself and your own family relationships. I know of no way to teach you to do that. Pray! As much as anything else, I suspect we each need to hear God's Spirit grant us permission to temporarily lay some of the load aside. Your care and nourishment for God's children must include yourself. You still have a lot to do.

4

The Funeral

By the time you get home it is too late to go back to bed.
You'd probably not sleep if you did. Too much is on your
mind.

You will try for the next two or three days to keep up with all
the rest of your responsibilities while you also fit in preparation
for the funeral or memorial service.

Caring Christian lay people are greatly needed during the
days ahead. Errands may need to be done. But don't push.
Some folks prefer to keep busy and do for themselves. However, if help is offered, Helen might plead, "Could *somebody*
take little Danny for a haircut?" Meals will need to be prepared
and served, and dishes will need to be washed. Transportation
may be needed for family members arriving from out of town.
Fred's brother is flying in, and his sister and her two children
are coming in by bus. Some churches have a standing com-
mittee available to try to meet the needs of the grieving family
during those several days of chaos. I have found it interesting
to note how often I later hear such comments as, "I never
knew how many people cared about us until now. It seems
that everybody has wanted to give something of themselves.
There is no way even to begin to express my feelings of gratitude."

The pastor should have assured Mrs. Jackson that he would
call at a certain time to help make plans for the funeral. Helen
needs to know as quickly as possible when he will or will not
be available for the funeral service. If his schedule is crowded,

the latter is urgent. Some people feel that the funeral must be held entirely at the convenience of the mortician. I'm not suggesting stubbornness, but I am suggesting coordination. Many ministers have heavy obligations, too. Of course, the smoothest cooperation is usually possible within the context of friendly relationships. Get acquainted with those with whom you likely will be working. That includes the mortician.

Because many friends who would like to attend but cannot afford the loss of a day's pay, the night funeral seems to be gaining in popularity in some places. It is an option worthy of consideration.

Some families like to have their minister with them when all funeral arrangements are made—including the casket selection. Others want only the most intimate members of the family. If they want you there, they will ask you. This is a delicate, painful time that calls for important financial decisions when they are emotionally least prepared to make them wisely. If guilts are strong in relation to the dead, a funeral that is economically beyond their means can easily become an atoning sacrifice. "I didn't do enough for him when he was alive. At least I can provide the very best (which often means the most costly) now that he is dead." *The wise minister will offer advice only if he is asked for it.* This general subject should have been addressed long ago from the pulpit to the whole congregation. People should have learned before this moment that the only adequate atonement was made almost two thousand years ago by Jesus Christ upon the cross. Their debt is paid in full—if they accept it.

Whether emotional, or social, or whatever, many experience tremendous pressures in selecting the casket and burial clothing, and in making other funeral-related decisions. A growing number of churches has reduced many of these pressures by returning to a tradition of earlier centuries, the purchase and use of a pall.

What is that? many would ask. A pall is a heavy cloth, usually black, gray, purple, or burgundy, large enough to drape the entire coffin. It is usually adorned with the symbol of the cross, a cross and crown combination, or with some other symbol of the Christian faith. The military funeral uses the flag as a pall. Covering the casket in the sanctuary and at the grave-side, the pall eliminates the social-economic pressure calling for an expensive casket and eliminates the need for a large, expensive floral blanket.

Let's face it. The major difference between a $1,000 funeral and a $10,000 funeral is the casket. The solid bronze casket may have its other qualities, but ultimately, it is seen as the way to "go out in style." With all else that may be said, its major purpose is to impress. The pine box is left for the pauper.

Having done a lot of listening across the years, I am convinced that few people attend a funeral who are not somewhat aware of the economic status reflected in the evident cost of the coffin. The pall reminds us that all are equal before God. The totally covered casket leaves minds less distracted and more free to meditate on higher values and greater concerns. After the burial, the funeral director can return the pall to the church, or it may be picked up at the mortuary.

Every geographic region seems to have its own customs that dictate what is considered "appropriate" during the next few days. Since custom often carries the force of law, if you are new to the area, you must get a thorough "briefing" from some well-experienced person in that locale. Pastors who have served in that region for several years and the local morticians are usually good resources. Otherwise, you are in danger of violating an established tradition—which some will consider irreverent and inexcusable. People in some locales still hold a wake which the minister is expected to visit. Some have never even heard of a wake (a continuous watch over the body until burial). Some church families will prepare meals and bring them to the home. Others will serve the family a meal at the church on the day of the funeral. Some will expect the minister at the first noon meal. Others will expect him for the evening meal. Others will see him as an intruder at any meal. The simple point is that local custom dictates what is expected of you before, during, and after the funeral.

If you are asked to have any part in the funeral, ask the family exactly what they expect of you. Though the pastor may assume he will have the leading role, including the meditative thought, many will expect that of the visiting minister. Surely that choice ought to be the family privilege. (I have seen as many as seven ministers have a part in a funeral.) Some will expect the pastor to assign ministerial responsibilities. Some families will want to do that assigning. Others will expect the participating ministers to "just know" what they are to do. Breaking their expectations at a time when feelings are sensitive will almost always cause problems later. If I seem to have belabored this point, it is for a good reason. Throughout the many years I have been in the ministry, I believe I've heard more criticism about what ministers did or did not do during the first week after a death than about any other subject.

Soon after the death the minister will call on the family, but he is there for a visit and not to take up residence for the next few days. (One dictionary defines *visit*: "to go to see briefly to give comfort or help.") How much time to spend with the family at this time is only one of the dilemmas facing the minister during these days. They may all center around the question, "What will be helpful or appropriate to their need?" All you do should then be consistent with your understanding of the answer to that question. But do not pull yourself into family affairs. Do they have favorite Scripture passages to include? What plans should be made for music? Solos? A small group? Congregational hymns? Organ music only? Do they want the funeral to be held in the mortuary chapel or at the church?

Though the trend in recent years has been toward the mortuary chapel, my experience suggests that most pastors are convinced that the church building is the most appropriate place for the Christian funeral. Any time the issue is raised for discussion, someone will contend that having the funeral in the church sanctuary will create problems for the family. Supposedly, they will be reminded of the funeral each time they return to that place of worship. Many of us immediately will counter that the place of worship is one of the most appropriate places to deal with grief. The unfamiliarity of the funeral chapel of the mortuary provides fewer resources. There is less of the familiar on which to draw strength, courage, and comfort. As one man put it, "When someone I love dies, as deeply as I love, I will need every resource I can find. I want every symbol and every memory of the highest of my worship experiences available to see me through. I know that one place is the sanctuary of my church where I worship regularly."

If, however, the attendance at the funeral is expected to be small, a near-empty church building may leave some families uncomfortable. Such matters need to be open to discussion. The decision must be theirs. Our purpose is to minister.

In his book *The Minister and Grief*, Robert W. Bailey has given the best discussion of the *Christian* funeral that I have seen. He points to four significant purposes of the funeral. He reminds us that the funeral provides a distinct time for mourning in which the bereaved clearly faces his loss. The Christian funeral also encourages openness to the love of God. It will reassure the survivors that God has not abandoned them. He is still caring for them even when they are angry with him. Since much of the pain endured at a funeral is in the tangible evidence of each person's own mortality, the Christian funeral provides a bridge over the fear of death by testifying to the resurrection and to life eternal with God. In addition to these, Bailey reminds his readers,

> Of all the reasons for a funeral, the central one is the opportunity for encountering God in worship. . . . A well-designed order of worship that includes great music of the church, appropriate Scripture, and a brief meditation can help transform a distressed person.[1]

God's recreative work goes on. *Plan to make the funeral truly an important worship experience!* Do family members have biblical readings they feel would be helpful to them? By the selection of passages of Scripture that point to the majesty of a loving and caring God, and by selection of great hymns of faith, the Christian funeral indeed can be an encounter with God where the grieving also find love and support from Christian brothers and sisters. Even the grieving should have the privilege, if they desire, to sing with the rest of the congregation (through their tears if necessary) "Guide Me, O Thou Great Jehovah" or "O God, Our Help in Ages Past." Though I am not a musician, I long ago recognized that while one may sing because his spirits are high, another should sing to get the spirit lifted.

Not every family will prefer a full congregational participation funeral, but many who are offered the opportunity welcome it. As is so often the case, such matters should be brought to people's minds from the pulpit by their pastors long before the immediate need. I have listened to a lot of preaching, but I have never heard a message that seemed intended to help families prepare for the funerals they will have to experience in their lives. Many plans can be made in advance. What cemetery will be used? Or will there be a cemetery?

For ecological, financial, aesthetic, and various individual reasons, the trend seems to be moving more and more toward cremation as a method of disposing of the body. It also has a stamp of finality that emphasizes the fact that the person is truly gone. The minister must be careful not to try to press his own feeling-laden preferences on those to whom he is there to serve. The Bible puts little emphasis on these matters. Early Christians seem to have had little concern for whether their bodies were burned or eaten by animals or otherwise disposed of. They had no further use for earthly habitation. God would provide whatever they needed for heaven.

Everyone seems to have feelings about the "opening of the casket" and the "viewing of the remains." I'm probably like many other people. I want to believe my position is based on rational thinking rather than on feeling alone. In earlier pages, I suggested a value in permitting the family to see the body just after a death. The value remains. Other members of the family who were not present at the time of the death may also wish to see the body to help finalize the relationship. And friends may have a similar need. The ties of friendship are sometimes stronger and deeper than those of family. The open casket at the mortuary and at the church *can* help these mourners too. But this is a *family* decision and should be made without the minister's suggestion unless he's asked to give it.

On the day of the funeral, unfortunately, many ministers will not see the family until they arrive at the funeral. Members of families, however, generally seem to appreciate a brief visit in the home about an hour before the service is due to begin. He can inquire of any last minute requests of the family and of their well-being. He can assure them again of God's love and of his own prayers in their behalf. He may remind them that their Christian friends are praying for them also. After the brief visit, he can lead them in prayer and leave with reassurance that he will look forward to ministering to them in the hour to come.

The funeral is something many people would like to avoid, but feel they have to go through with it. Keep it short. Few will truly hear what you have to say. When people are in intense grief, their attention span for *anything* but their loss may be *no more than a few seconds at a time*. The drama of the funeral ritual usually intensifies the feelings of grief. This means that at best, they will each get only a few brief "glimpses" of the truths of which you speak or read. Some ministers give the family a typed copy of the funeral sermon. Since the advent of the small cassette recorder, many ministers have found that families appreciate having the message recorded. At a later time, when they are emotionally better prepared to hear what was said, they may listen without the external pressures. But give it to them only if they want it.

As I have already indicated, brevity should describe every

part of the funeral service—brief prayers, brief passages of Scripture, and a brief message. Ask people their preference. You will find that just about everyone feels the funeral for someone in their family should be about twenty minutes. And never more than thirty, including time for all music.

Unfortunately, those who need to hear this the most will probably never read it, and if they do, they will scoff. I know of one funeral message that went on and on and on for an hour and a half. The funeral director finally closed the casket and began to usher the people out while the man kept on preaching. Some of my friends were subjected to two one-hour sermons at the church and a third one-hour sermon at the graveside. It is still a subject that arouses anger when they talk of it after several years. They gained the distinct feeling that the preachers were competing with one another.

The funeral has one primary purpose—to minister to the family. The word was *minister*—not *impress*. That may be the effort if a guest of importance is there. Since God is there, how much more important a guest can you have? Serve him by serving his hurting children. Try to determine the needs of the family and use the experience to serve those needs. What truths will help to bring healing to that which is broken within them? Such healing will not come from an elaborate eulogy!

I attended a funeral not long ago in which fourteen minutes were devoted to the greatness of the dead man and three minutes to the greatness of God. (I timed it.) Something was far out of proportion! That was a time when the children came asking for bread and were handed a stone. Of course, you should use the person's name at some time during the service but beware of many elevating words no matter how great you and the world saw him to be. The jokes I've heard across the years about ministers "preaching men into heaven" at the funeral have all been sick. Every one of them holds the minister up to derision. The family *knows* what kind of a person he was. Leave *all* final judgments to God. They have lived with him behind closed doors. They could tell you some things—

both good and bad. Help them to gain strength from God instead of from their memories of the deceased. It is God who has the power to sustain them across the years ahead. When hearts are down, help them to find the courage to look up and behold the Lord.

People sometimes "borrow" on our faith. Your confident assertion of religious truth is often received as, "I'm not sure I believe that, but, since you are confident, I'll accept it as valid for now." Even beyond your words, people sense your feeling of hope or despair. They "borrow on your faith" that *death is not the end* (unless you do not have a confident hope and expectation of life beyond this life). You are not there to argue for eternal life but to affirm it. For the one who has died, death is no tragedy! The tragedy is in the loss for those who remain behind. Death to the Christian is a door necessary for transition from one state of awareness to the next—from one abiding place to the next. As one man said recently, "For *my* sake I'd give anything to have my father back, but for *his* sake I wouldn't bring him back if I could." Most of our desire to have them back grows out of one of two things—selfishness, or lack of confidence that they are better off in the presence of God in heaven.

You may be asking, but what of the non-Christian? Unfortunately, I have little to offer. I can offer nothing the Scriptures do not seem to offer. Ministers have few chores more uncomfortable than the funeral of someone they clearly view as an unbeliever. None seem to suffer more than those of the family who look up from their tears and cry, "Nothing about his life suggests he ever trusted God for *anything* at any time." I can only insist that we leave all judgment to God and assure the grieving that God will walk with them *through* the valley of the shadow of death. He will not leave them nor forsake them, no matter what they feel.

Just as the funeral is no time to "preach people into heaven," neither is it the time to "preach people into hell." Proclaim the greatness of God and leave judgment to him. I am not likely ever to forget the words of a woman who seemed to be working hard to destroy herself by partaking of every immorality within her reach. "When Daddy died, the preacher said Daddy had gone to hell. I loved my daddy so much, and wanted to be with him so much, I decided to make sure I went to hell, too." Her own judgment and life-style proclaimed that she had indeed, made a "hell on Earth" for herself.

Whether you view the dead as saint or sinner, magnify the greatness and love of God as one who cares deeply for those who remain to live. The most difficult time may yet be ahead. In a traditional funeral of this era, the body still must be buried.

The graveside service for many is the worst time of all. The local mortician and experienced pastors in the area can help you to know the local traditions for this service, too. For instance, some may expect you to walk slowly ahead of those who carry the casket from the hearse to the grave. Traditions vary. Get the family's approval before you violate their tradition in any way.

With the casket suspended above a six-foot hole in the ground, about to be lowered and covered with dirt, the family usually wishes to endure no more at the graveside than a brief passage of Scripture and brief prayer.

Immediately following this service, many want to leave, but others are accustomed to milling about the cemetery, quietly talking with friends and family. While some will think me foolish for suggesting the most obvious, others will see the violation so minor that it is not worth mentioning. But I offer a warning. If you can keep from doing so, *don't walk on the graves!* They may be the graves of former friends or the graves of former members of families present. You are going to offend some who will become convinced that you have no "respect for the dead." (And I have to admit that I'm not even sure I understand all that is implied by "respect" or lack of "respect" for the dead.)

During this time of quiet conversation, workmen may be filling the grave. Those closest to the deceased often pretend they are unaware of what is going on. For some, it is their darkest hour. When the chore is complete, many want to visit the spot one last time before departure. That ugly mound of dirt may be covered with an artificial grass carpet and flowers, but the pain of loss cannot be covered. It can only be endured. Do not be offended if people want to be completely alone in these moments. Throughout their grief, many periodically wish to withdraw. They may be talking to themselves. They may be talking to God, or they may be talking to the dead. We will probably always struggle within ourselves to determine when we are needed and when we may be hovering too near. We don't want to smother them in any way. Trying to rely on both common sense and the leadership of God, we will still sometimes make mistakes. Even these mistakes are easier to accept by those to whom we minister if we have not tried to make ourselves appear without error before this time.

Helen Jackson and the children have had a difficult time during the last few days. You may want to walk from the graveside back to the car in which she will be riding home, unless this task is being taken care of by family members or intimate friends. You will probably leave a few minutes ahead of them.

And most grieving people are left at this point to endure their loss alone with no one to minister to them as they struggle to adjust during the months or years ahead.

5

After The Funeral

Our most important ministry to the bereaved may yet lie in the future. But a survey reported by Charles Bachmann suggests that with the possible exception of one postfuneral call, few people will receive any grief ministry once they walk away from the grave.[1] Though I have some difficulty fully interpreting Bachmann's study, a ministudy by Gay Harris, who served as a regional chaplain for a chain of seven funeral homes for three years, fully supports Bachmann. Harris says that his records show 40 percent of the people in his region died without affiliation with any local church body. Without exception, those who used the services of a "borrowed pastor" never again after the funeral received a contact from the pastor or from the church he served.

We would like to grant that those ministers knew of the chaplain's services and left the follow-up ministry to him. The remainder of his study discourages us from that conclusion. Of the 60 percent who were members of a church, one of each four had one pastoral visit after the day of the funeral. Not one received a second. That means that 75 percent of those who had a pastor did not receive even one follow-up pastoral visit. And the 25 percent who had a pastoral visit received one and no more. Boiling that down to its simplest form, his findings tell us that during the three years of his study, only fifteen families of each one hundred had even one pastoral visit following the funeral of a loved one.

Bachmann's national survey and Harris's study in a large

Southern US city seem to arrive at the same conclusion. Few people receive any grief ministry after the day of the funeral.

Reflection may lead us to wonder if this has any effect on our credibility when we try to evangelize. It is sometimes hard for us to convince people that God cares when they feel we do not care. We might also wonder if our neglect of a follow-up grief ministry may be one of the primary reasons many people leave the church within six months after the death of a close family member. They feel abandoned. Indeed, many *are* abandoned. But they still need a ministry.

The first time the family walks back into the house after the funeral, they may experience pain like they have never known before. All but the very closest will usually have gone their separate ways. The aloneness and the emptiness of the house often begin here. The minister, waiting in the driveway to accompany the family into the house, will probably be a welcome sight. For many, it will be the first time they will have begun to relax and to think aloud. Listen! They are tired. The drain has been physical as well as emotional. They probably will have gone to bed late every night since the death. The coming and going of friends, though appreciated, will have taken its toll. They are weary. Their thoughts and their words at this time are important. Hear them carefully. People tend to lower their guard when they are tired. Their failures, their pain, and their dread of the future may get put into words more clearly than at any time before. A lot needs to be said and heard. But do not stay too long. If you really want an effective ministry to the bereaved, you will be back. At best, recovery will have just begun. Have prayer and let them know you will return in a few days.

Few people seem prepared for what is highly probable from within two or three days up to two or three weeks: *a fresh, huge, wave of depression.* Right after they learned of the death, they went into a valley of darkness but probably began to come out within a few days. It was at this point that most friends and relatives left them, assuming all was well and that they were into the process of recovery. But many, and maybe most, begin to experience a new low, even more intense than the original.

After several days, it often begins to "soak in" that their loved one really is gone and will not be coming back. Fred Jackson and millions of others have had the practice of leaving town from time to time for professional or personal reasons. Their families have grown accustomed to being without them for a few days at a time. One day they awaken and realize the loved one really isn't coming back again. We aren't talking about logic now. We are talking about a *feeling,* an awareness of reality. The initial shock may have been so great that Helen was not able to feel the extent of her true loss. A growing awareness begins. All she can see are his clothes in the closet, his shoes under the bed, and his screwdriver on the bench where he left it. She passes his dresser and smells his after-shaving lotion. She reaches for him in the night and awakens because he's not there. She wants to scream because *he won't ever be there again.*

A ministerial visit within two or three days after the funeral is urgent. (Make sure the children are at home or have someone with you.) Many who try to work closely in the process of grief recovery insist that a minimum of four to six (separate) hours of quiet conversation with the minister are needed by anyone who has lost a loved one. If these few hours were routinely offered, our mental hospitals would be far less crowded, and we would need far fewer in the various psychotherapeutic fields of service! I am saying that unresolved grief is one of the major contributing factors in the mental illness in our culture today!

Edgar Jackson has probably done more than any other writer to help those of us in the therapeutic professions to understand the problems of grief. In *Understanding Grief* he urges that the grieving be encouraged to talk through their grief and reminds us that "ancient Jewish custom allowed for a week of mourning during which the bereaved and his friends were allowed to talk only about the deceased."[2] *We should be so wise!* We more typically allow three days to get the body in the ground and dare the family members to talk about their loved one any longer than the time it takes for a tear to begin to form before we change the subject! Allow them—*encourage* them to talk about their dead loved one.

On that first visit in the home after the day of the funeral, I suggest you take a small book. Granger Westburg's *Good Grief* is my own preference. One of my associates prefers *Tracks of a Fellow Struggler* by John Claypool. Others prefer Edgar Jackson's *You and Your Grief.* Take your pick of one. All are small, inexpensive, and worth purchasing in quantity to have available to *give* to families in grief. You may want to make a personal inscription. At least have copies in the church library to lend. They inform, and they stimulate conversation. Use no book as an excuse to cut back on your personal ministry. Use it as a tool to broaden your ministry. Ask Helen to read the book and tell her that you wish to return within a week to discuss what she has read and anything else that the reading may have stirred within her. (Of course, that means you will be well acquainted with the book too.) You may find it best to make a specific appointment to come back or to meet her in your office. Keep the children included.

That first week after the funeral tends to be rather hectic for the immediate family. Insurance policies seem never to be where they are supposed to be. Bank accounts usually have to be changed. Some may have been frozen, making the money unavailable until the will has been probated. If Fred had failed to make a will, Helen's additional problems would be too numerous to describe. But they still have to find the birth certificate, and have to get a death certificate. In fact, she will probably need *several* copies. The probate judge will want a copy to be filed with the will. Each life insurance claim will require a copy. Indeed, practically every legal transaction growing out of Fred's death will require a copy of the death certificate. Helen will have enough financial and legal problems to keep her occupied for several days, but unless you are truly a specialist in such matters, *don't advise*. But know those who are specialists and can advise. Let Helen know that you will be available to direct her to those who can help her if she needs it.

Encourage Helen and the children to be in church the very next Sunday. Their lives will be enriched, and the congregation will be glad to have the opportunity to minister to them. Ask the family to come to your study before the worship service for a time of prayer.

Most people are not prepared for the additional losses they begin to experience almost immediately. Helen will probably lose her sense of "belonging." She will no longer be a part of her former social sphere. The "unattached" woman is a threat to a lot of wives. They fear she is out to "get their man." The widow of a man of any degree of prominence in the community immediately loses the status she has enjoyed by way of association. Millions of women lose their economic security with the death of their husbands. She has to adjust to these problems and more.

Obviously, I am urging a strong *ongoing* ministry for as long as she and the children have the need. The degree to which she authorizes you to minister to her and her family will usually depend on the relationship you had with them before the tragedy. The warmth of the relationship is urgent. If Fred had died after a lingering illness and you failed to minister regularly to her and her dying husband, you could not expect to be permitted to minister to her now. Make an occasional phone call. In quiet pastoral conversations with her, make specific inquiries, "Helen, what difficulties are you meeting in adjusting to Fred's death?"

Many of her friends are afraid even to mention his name. If you are uncomfortable about speaking his name, ask how she feels about your doing so.

Helen still has three children to parent, and someone probably will tell her that she now has to be both mother and father to them. You may have to remind her that she can't do that. (The pulpit would have been an excellent place to deal with that sort of problem, long before Fred's death.) There is just not enough of her to fill both roles. She is destined to frustration, failure, and guilt. No person can truly fill the roles of both father and mother. Just as she has to do without a husband for now, her three children will have to do without a father. Her task is to try to be a good mother to them. That is a big job within itself! She has enough guilt feelings without this being added. Encourage her to deal with one problem at a time.

She was not a perfect wife. Of course, Fred wasn't a perfect husband. They were a perfectly normal couple. She will tend to remember her failures to be as good a wife as she feels she ought to have been. She may glorify Fred for some time to come. Looking too closely at his imperfections may stir too much guilt. If it tends to stir up any anger, she will probably feel guilty for feeling anger against the dead. After all, he can't defend himself now.

She has another source of inner distress that few women are prepared to meet. Some men of the community are absolutely convinced that any woman who is without a man is burning with passion with no way to satisfy her needs. Each one is sure he is God's gift to lonely, hungry women, and each is eager to relieve her distress. She is likely to be propositioned from the most unexpected sources. Fred's best friend, and her best friend's husband may be at the head of the line. If she is only outraged, she is fortunate. If she is somewhat naive, she may feel terribly guilty—wondering if she is suddenly giving off some sort of mysterious "vibes" that scream to men, "I'm available." By the time she does begin to feel some need, she may feel guilty and cheap for having the very normal feminine interests aroused. If she does fall into some sexual indiscretion, she may feel additional guilt. Offer her no excuses and no justifications. Give her no judgment! Point her to the forgiving grace of our Lord Jesus Christ, whether for that which you consider major moral violations or for those you consider far less serious.

For instance, she may feel terribly guilty because she has trouble remembering what he looked like. Why do you think so many people keep the photographs of their loved ones around? Many are terrified that they will forget the face of their loved one. "Surely I wouldn't really forget. That must mean I didn't really love him." Some will feel guilty because they feel they do not hurt as much as they ought to hurt after such a loss. No matter how little sense it makes to you, we are talking about real human struggle and pain. Keep on listening patiently and compassionately.

You may need to remind her to be patient with herself. An important part of her has been cut off. Many people believe they should return to normal within a few weeks at most. In reality, few people recover within six months, and most will need from one to three years. A few will need more. Those who would criticize the length of another's grief need to hear the words of Richard Baxter, who was criticized by his friends for grieving too long over the death of his wife. "I will not be judged by those who have never known the like."[3] His trace of anger is far milder than some would express amid their pain.

The loss of a loved one sometimes has been likened to a major amputation. We would not expect an immediate recovery if Helen had lost a limb of her body. Fred's death was the loss of no less an integral part of her than her leg. In fact, she might tell you that the loss of a leg or arm would have been less painful. Even after that one-to-three-year period of adjustment, the pain may return as an unexpected ocean wave. The notes of a song, the whiff of an old fragrance, the sound of a voice, the back of a head, the sparkle in a stranger's eye, or any number of a thousand personal events may revive the old grief at the most unexpected times. But some can be predicted.

Just as most people keep up with the birthdays in their family, they also tend to remember their "death dates." Those ministers who want to serve their people during their difficult times will keep up with the death dates also. Keep a file, or keep a well-marked calendar. But no matter how you do it, keep up with the anniversary dates of the deaths within those families you serve. A ministerial visit in the home *exactly* one year after Fred's death should hold a near top priority in your ministry. Helen will be aware of the date. The children probably will too. They will have a lot of memories stirred. Not only will it be of value for them to talk freely, but they will be pleasantly surprised that their minister has also kept up with the date and is trying with compassion to reach out to them. They will be comforted to know that God's representative cares enough to concern himself with such matters.

And no matter how well they have adjusted to Fred's death, for at least the next two years you should visit in the home or call by phone on the anniversary of Fred's death. "I am aware that Fred died two years ago today. I just wanted to call to see how things are going for you and the children." Your call is not going to remind them of something they are trying to forget. They're already remembering. And you should not stop your ministry here. People have their grief stirred afresh at other predictable times also. Helen and Fred's wedding anniversary date may be a difficlt time. Thanksgiving and Christmas are family holidays for many. They each open the door to fresh pain.

You probably are viewing one of the biggest concerns a pastor must face. Even the most caring pastor cannot provide all the ministry these and other occasions demand. For this reason, many churches have adopted a program of organized lay ministry. In such a program, every "ministering deacon," "lay volunteer," or "trained lay workman" (or whatever the title) should maintain a file of significant dates in the lives of those to whom he or she is to minister. Such churches will want to make sure that Helen and her children are assigned for ongoing care. (I was in the pulpit of a church recently and mentioned their strong program of ministering deacons. I was astonished by a rousing *applause!* That church and pastor are *proud* of their deacons.)

I recommend personal contacts on or near these dates I just mentioned for at least the first three years after a death. In addition, the pastor will do well to remember the grieving in his public prayers during the traditional holiday seasons. And an occasional sermon for the grieving will be especially well timed at the holiday seasons. Not only is the pain intense, some of the problems initiated by a death are large.

The loss of a loved one creates more problems for the typical person than almost any other experience. And one particular loss seems to stand out above all others—the death of a child. We would like to believe that the mutual loss of a child by a mother and father will somehow lock them together in a more permanent bond than ever before. But Compassionate Friends, a self-help organization of bereaved parents with United States headquarters at PO Box 1374, 800 Enterprise Drive, Oakbrook, Illinois, 60521, estimates that as many as 90 percent of all couples in bereavement are having serious marital difficulties within months after the death of their child. (Harriett Schiff, author of the book *The Bereaved Parent* [Crown, 1977] agreed.) Divorce is likely for as many as 70 percent. Each tends to feel the other locks them to the past and to the dead child. Tied to one another, they feel tied inescapably to their grief.

The psychosocial dynamics are far too multiple and complicated to pursue here. That is beyond the scope of this "how-to-minister" material. Those who study it say it is the most persistent and intense of all grief. I have personally seen grief linger for more than forty years after a child's death. We must be patient, loving, compassionate, and ready to recommend the best marriage counselor we know.

Let's look at some of the symptoms of problems that we should watch for in the lives of any who grieve.

Watch for what you think seems to be an unreasonable

withdrawal. People who are adjusting healthily will be returning to their normal level of *functioning* within a month or less.
They will be able to carry on their work, or their studies, and
their social interaction, in spite of their preoccupation with
their loss. If they are still going down after a month, they probably are going to need some outside help by the services of an
experienced pastoral counselor or other Christian therapist.

If their whole meaning for life has been wrapped up in the
loved one, listen carefully for withdrawal wishes that suggest
suicide. Keep in mind also that the man over sixty-five, in poor
health, who recently has lost his wife, is the most likely candi-
date for suicide among us today. In addition to the loneliness
and the loss of meaning to life, some wish to die so they can
be reunited with their dead loved ones.

But Helen is rather young and has small children. And they
may be her biggest concern. Without a father in the home, she
may have a problem with authority. Young boys often want to
assume the departed father's role, trying to take it as though it
came as an inheritance. When this happens, we see a not-so-
subtle power struggle within the home. If the attitude were
actually spoken, she might hear, "I'm the seat of authority in
this home now. How dare you try to exercise authority over
me?" Coupled with this highly complicated psychological dy-
namic, or independent of it, Helen may be facing another
problem to which we who minister to her family should be
alert.

Be watchful for any change in the pattern of the children's
behavior. Of course, this is one of the advantages of an ongoing family ministry—you know them over an extended
period of time. You have known the Jackson family as having
"pretty good kids." If, after their father's death (or the death of
anyone they have loved), they turn to delinquent, degrading
behavior, or behavior that tends to get them in trouble with the
law enforcement authorities, you can be almost assured they
are "acting out" their unresolved grief over the death of their
father. It probably will be their expression of anger or guilt. It

may be both. The more of it they are able to put into words the less of it they are likely to put into damaging behavior. Be a good listener and try to "toughen your own hide." If you get close to them, and it is anger they feel, you may get the full blast of their rage. If you are not ready or able to absorb that, or you feel professionally inadequate to deal with it, be quick to recommend some *Christian* professional counselor (therapist). (Yes, I gave emphasis to the *Christian* orientation of the counselor. This is not the time nor the place to debate the "pros and cons" of a distinctively Christian counselor over against a counselor who is non-Christian. I will move on by pleading that you try to recommend only a counselor who works out of a commitment to God in Jesus Christ.)

It may not be just the children's behavior that changes. Helen's behavior may become "delinquent" too. She may need as much counseling as the children—maybe more.

Before we get too far from the problem of guilt again, let me point out a monumental source of it.

We tend to have a hard time letting ourselves reap any benefit from the death of someone we have loved. Before Fred died, almost daily, Helen felt the pressure of economic survival for her family. Not only did Fred's insurance pay off the mortgage on the house, but now money is in the bank assuring the children's college education. (Had it been one of the children who had died, they would have been relieved of the many economic and other responsibilities that parents have for their children.)

Since responsibility is carried as a weight upon us, no matter how voluntarily we carry it, when it is removed, we feel some sense of relief. That sense of relief tends to produce the sense of guilt. Helen is now relieved of the responsibilities to her husband, and because of Fred's insurance money she is relieved of the many economic pressures she has lived with for years. She tends to think to herself, *"How dare you receive any benefit from the death of the man you have loved—and look at that insurance money! You have actually profited by*

the death of the man you have loved. That's 'blood' money."
Our rationalizations, our justifications, our persuasions just
aren't going to help. She's heard them all in her own mind
long before she ever got the courage to come to you with her
struggle.

Accept it as a vote of confidence and a compliment if she
does turn to you with such guilt. Most who do ever deal with it
openly do so much later within the context of some larger gen-
eralized problem needing the services of a professional level of
counseling. I'm not suggesting that you need to be a professional counselor to help her deal with it. In fact, if she can
share it within a nonjudgmental, accepting, caring, compassionate atmosphere, if she has enough confidence in you to
know she will not be quoted (without permission), if she is
given the uninterrupted freedom to wander verbally through
the mental-emotional maze of thought and feeling, she may
never need that "professional" couselor. Your uncritical ac-
ceptance of her may help her to forgive herself and to accept
what God has for her amid the struggle.

Once again we are back to a subject that has recurred
throughout our examination of our ministry to the bereaved:
people's confidence in us who minister. If confidence in us is
so important, is there any way we can consciously and inten-
tionally work to build it in the people we would serve? Yes! It is
not just a matter of "personality" or a trait that we were "born
with." It's a quality to be learned and cultivated. People to
whom you reach out to minister are asking questions about
you. Before they give you their trust, you will stand a test.
Since every person who ministers must repeatedly stand this
examination, it may help to look at some of the questions they
are silently asking.

Can I trust him to keep quiet about what I tell him? If they
trust you to keep confidences, you have the struggle for their
trust half won. People want to know if we can "keep our
mouths shut" about the intimate matters in their lives. I recently heard a woman say, "I wouldn't tell my pastor anything!

He tells everything he knows right from the pulpit. When he starts telling some of his illustrations, I want to crawl under the pew. I know whom he is talking about, and I know that half the people in the church know, too." Confidences violated in one sermon illustration or in idle conversation may so damage the trust of a church that years may be required for recovery. Trust is always delicate and fragile and must be handled with care. It's valuable, sacred, and easily broken. People want to know that confidences will be guarded with reverence.

The struggle for people's confidence is sometimes best won by a direct, frontal attack. If you are worthy of their trust, tell them so! Tell them that confidences are sacred to you. I find that it is often helpful to assure someone who seems uneasy that nothing said will be repeated. Many have responded, "I felt that you wouldn't repeat what I tell you or I wouldn't be here, but thanks, I needed the reassurance too." My words not only give them reassurance, they give me a fresh promise to keep!

Helen may want you to talk with her son. You should respond, "I'll be glad to talk with your son, but whatever he says to me behind closed doors cannot be repeated even to you." Such comments tend to convey much about your attitude toward confidences. She is likely to conclude, "If my son's words are to be in confidence, mine probably will be in confidence too."

People tend to conduct this part of their test by degrees. They may tell a relatively unimportant secret and then wait to see what you do with it. If you are found faithful, they will share more and wait and watch again for evidences of your having violated their trust. Each bit of sharing usually gets deeper and more personal and more relaxed in freedom of expression. But their test of you is far from ended.

People are asking, *Can I trust him to let me make my own decisions?* Many who turn to the minister are not sure of themselves. They have made mistakes. Many have tried to live up to everybody's expectation. Of course, they've failed. They feel inadequate to make significant decisions. If Fred was a

husband who trusted Helen with few decisions, she will almost
surely feel inadequate. But decision making is an important
aspect in the process of human growth. Practice is necessary,
and one has to take the risk and the responsibility upon himself for incorrect decisions. One also needs the joy and satisfaction that is the reward for correct decisions. When the minister tries to make a decision for someone, he is agreeing, "I,
also, think you are too inadequate to live your own life." This
attitude is only thinly veiled when it comes out, "I wouldn't
think of telling you what to do, but if I were in your situation, I
would. . . ." Many who come to us are confused, but few are
stupid.

A part of the struggle to make one's own decisions forms an
additional test question: *Will I be rejected by the minister if I
make a decision with which the minister does not agree?*

As a part of their venture to trust us, they are also asking,
Can I trust him to withhold judgment? One of the greatest
drawbacks people have, in taking concerns to the minister, is
the fear of his condemnation. "He might criticize me." Or,
"I'm afraid I'll lose esteem in his eyes." Or, "I'm afraid he
won't think as highly of me as I want him to think." Or, in
short, "Will he withdraw his love and respect if he sees the real
me?" While confession is among the great human needs, people are often terrified of the minister's judgment. His open
condemnation of others drives many to conclude, "If I were to
let him see my faults, he would condemn me, too." The frightening question then arises, "If you can't accept me, does
God?" If we do accept the person who has made mistakes,
that person will be closer to concluding, "God really does
accept me just as I am."

One may fear the minister's condemnation of someone else
that is loved. A man came seeking aid in his struggle to rebuild
a marriage relationship. "Before I could come to you I had to
know if I could trust you not to take sides. My wife has hurt me
by doing something you probably judge as wrong; but I still
love her, and I don't want you to criticize her. We need to talk

with someone who won't take sides with either of us." If Helen felt the need to share something negative about Fred, she doesn't want you to judge him harshly—especially now that he is dead.

Continuing their efforts to trust us they ask, *Can I trust him to really care? Why is he so interested as I bare my soul? Is it really because he knows it may help me? Or is it just to satisfy some perverted, morbid sense of curiosity?* We may as well admit it. Not all voyeurs are hiding outside bedroom windows. "Peeping Tomism" may be practiced by any who reach out to help another. Every minister will do well to frequently examine his own motives for listening as those in distress unveil their most intimate thoughts.

Others are asking, *Does he care enough to really listen to me? Or will he interrupt just as I begin to open up and offer a too simple solution to my distress. Will he push me out the door telling me just to, "Pray about it and everything will work out all right?" Don't I have some part in solving the problems in my own life?*

People may also be wondering, *Can I trust him to take me seriously?* Most people have at least a few secret fears. They have thoughts, feelings, impulses, or urges that make them feel isolated and different from everyone else. They fear that the revelation of some of their secrets will evoke a laugh or a label of "crazy" from the minister. So Helen might sometimes have an urge to eat clay, or she occasionally sees a halo around certain persons. She may fear her own feelings of omnipotence (that her feelings of anger might have caused Fred's death just because she at one time had a fleeting wish for it).

Such thoughts may sound absurd to the minister, but a laugh at such matters may wound deeply. That which is brought to us as serious should be taken seriously.

A highly important question could easily be a part of Helen's concern if the one in the ministering role is a man: *Am I safe with him? Can I trust him not to hurt me?* The quest for a confidant is largely a quest for freedom. But it is often a frightening quest, because by unveiling, we pull down the defenses, making ourselves vulnerable. That is, we are opening ourselves to be hurt—by rejection, scorn, or something else. The wounds taken to the minister are not always fresh, but they are "raw" and sensitive.

Women ask, *Can I trust him with my feelings? Or will he take advantage of them?* This is one of those things that we would rather not admit but may as well face. Unfortunately, some ministers have gained questionable reputations. Every woman who approaches a minister with a concern has the right to be assured of safety.

Thus we arrive at one of the most significant questions of the examination. *Is this minister a "confidence man" or a man worthy of confidence?* If he's a "confidence man," he seeks to gain people's trust because he is "out for what he can get." If he's a man worthy of confidence, true to his calling, he seeks to gain people's trust because he is there for what he can give. It is in search of this difference that we who minister are examined. It just sounds too good to be true that the minister's struggle to gain people's confidence is only for the purpose of ministry. But may it ever be so.[4]

It is not only confidence in us that we are trying to cultivate, but we work to help build confidence in One far beyond ourselves. If we are trying to represent Christ and his church, those we face raise another important question: *Is there a word from the Lord?* Each of us who dares speak for him must speak of his saving work in all of life.

Not only does God provide a salvation that extends beyond the grave, he provides a multitude of saving works all along the way. One of the evidences of his saving grace is those he saves from the pit of despair following a death, even though that sometimes may be a terribly long, complicated process of healing. But like all his saving works, each person must accept it as his own if he is to reap the benefits. God seems always to give the right and privilege to every person to say no to any of his saving works. For reasons as individual as the fingerprints, some will hold to their grief for many years and some for a lifetime.

"God *will* take care of you" sounds good, but it may need a lot of interpretation. To Helen, those words may sound as though you are promising that God will protect her from all complication and pain. You may know that is unrealistic, but she may hear it and feel that God has let her down. You may mean that God will provide comfort and strength, but all of God's salvation is conditional. God's promises usually have an "if" in them. God refuses to force himself on anyone. He comes saying, "I will provide for you *if* you will accept what I have to give." *Not everyone accepts it!* Not all *can* accept it because of their own concept of him or because of their own particular relationship with him.

The person who stands in the pulpit, the ministering staff, yes, all the church have the opportunity, even the responsibility to reach out to a brother or a sister who is wounded by the painful events of life. But in *any* family, every person holds the right to reject or accept any love that is offered.

People of the church often have been called the "family of God"—a thoroughly biblical concept. God's Holy Spirit, personally, and through the church, nourishes and comforts. Among the individual members of the family of the church we find brothers and sisters who provide emotional and spiritual support, and who help to fill the void left by the dead loved one. The church can provide small groups where support can be given and with whom feelings can be worked through in an atmosphere of compassion.

Some churches have formalized and structured this ministry by establishing grief recovery groups—a form of group therapy. Since Christ's church is intended to be a nourishing, therapeutic community working to promote healing of persons, when equipped people are available, nothing could be more natural. Does your church have a dedicated clinical psychologist, or psychiatrist, or a social worker with training in the group process? Have you had Clinical Pastoral Education or do you have access to a CPE center or a nearby university in which you might get training in group work?

Do you have access to a committed Christian who might come to your church long enough to help get such a program on the move? For example, most states have a hundred or more chaplains with special training and are affiliated with almost every conceivable type of institution, civilian and military. Some have gone for years without ever having been invited to provide some ministry to those of the nearby churches. Many would be delighted to help set up a grief recovery program. (See the Appendix for suggestions for establishing a grief recovery group.)

A part of Helen's grief has come from the loss of someone to whom she could give. The giving of her time and effort through the social ministries of the church provide something far more worthwhile than just "keeping busy." It helps her to maintain a purpose and provides a way to direct her grief toward some positive end. It provides a fresh outlet for her to "lose her grief" in unselfish service to others in need.[5] "There is no better armor against the shafts of death than to be busied in God's service," said Thomas Fuller.[6]

Virtually every service agency in every city has a need for volunteer help. If the first you contact does not, it can point you to others who do. If you make a few calls, you will be more knowledgeable of the local needs, and you will help her to find an opportunity for meaningful service to others wounded by life's experiences. You may find that your area has a published directory of service agencies. Even the compilers are often surprised by the large number they find. About any agency you contact will know how to get a copy of that directory. Thank God for each one of them and for the people who function within them. Each was established to serve people with a particular kind of human pain. But those who grieve are left to the ministry of the church.

You have known many who suffer the pains of grief, and by

the time you finish your ministry, you probably will have known a lot more. Each time you consent to walk in the valleys of sorrow with those you serve, you feel a pain within your own soul. The hurts of others hurt you. That which you bear makes the load just a little lighter for those you serve. When you have so denied yourself, having taken up your cross and having followed in the path of our Lord Jesus, if you will listen carefully, you just may hear a quietly whispered, "Well done, thou good and faithful servant. . . . Enter thou into the joy of thy lord" (Matt. 25:21).

Christ's whole church was intended to be a healing community. With compassion, patient understanding, service, and love, the church—the body of Christ—will continue to promote healing to the soul. Then Helen and her children, and all those of the fellowship who grieve, may once again freely lift their hearts and sing, "My God, How Great Thou Art!"[7]

Appendix

Loss Recovery

Dr. Howard Clinebell, several years ago, established the concept of the church-centered "Grief Recovery Group."[1] After listening to him, I established a similar program but expanded the concept to a "Loss Recovery Group." It has some distinct advantages. It provides a ministry to more than those who hurt only from the loss of a loved one in death. And since many smaller churches would have relatively few grieving a death at one time, the broader loss recovery group is more practical for a small church but is no less effective in a large church.

The loss recovery group ministers to that part of the fellowship of a church hurting from *any* loss in their lives that still evokes enough pain to be considered problematic. Most of life's greatest pain follows a loss of some kind. If it is not the loss of someone in death, it is the loss of health, the loss of youth, or the loss of a job. It may be the loss of a dream, or the loss of status, or the loss of one's self-respect. These, and a lot more, are losses that create sufficient inner conflict to warrant a ministry.

The pain often lingers for a matter of years, draining the ability to live life to its fullest. If a man loses a leg, he is crippled. If he loses a wife in death, or his productivity in retirement, he may also be crippled. They are all grief-producing experiences! Accurately defined, grief is the response one has to the loss of that which he loves. What I suggest, therefore, is still a grief recovery group but using a different name to keep from sounding as though it were limited only to those recovering from loss by death.

Initiation

Coordinate the beginning time, date, and place of meeting with other church leaders.

Make the first announcement six weeks before starting to give everyone ample opportunity to think about individual needs, and to ask any questions that come to mind.

Use all methods of communication within the church: bulletin, newsletter, bulletin board, announcement period at the hour of worship, and so forth.

Suggested Sample Announcement

On Sunday evening, April 19, one hour and thirty minutes prior to the time of worship, a loss recovery group will be established to help the membership of this church to minister more fully to its people. Using many of the principles of group therapy, its purpose is to quicken the healing process for those who have been wounded by any loss and are still hurting from that loss, no matter how old or recent the loss.

If you have lost someone you loved, a job, or the ability to bear a child, or if you have had any other loss with which you continue to struggle, here you may find help for yourself as you help others in the group. Think in terms of a commitment of each Sunday evening for eight weeks. *Mr. John Smith,* who is trained in the principles of group encounter, will be leading. The rest of the church is asked to remember this group in prayer.

First Encounter

If there is any possibility that all members do not know one another, make name tags for all. These should be filled out as participants arrive and should be left behind at the end of the meeting for use from week to week.

Chairs should be placed in a tight circle, close enough for knees or elbows to occasionally brush together. Even with name tags in place, all should be asked to introduce themselves to the group.

The group leader should offer prayer immediately after introductions. He should give a brief statement of purpose and method with discussion of the need for confidence to be maintained by all involved. He will make a pledge of confidence and ask for it from the members. At this point, the leader should say something to this effect:

> We will now join hands, bow our heads, close our eyes, and remember. That word *remember* carries the idea of "bringing back to life." We are going to bring back to life our *thoughts and feelings* about our loss that still hurt us. We are going to concentrate on taking ourselves back to live the experience again, with all the feelings of hurt, loss, anger, guilt, emptiness, frustration, and any other feelings that were there. Go back to the moments you first got the idea of what was about to happen. How did you feel when you realized it was inevitable? [Talk slowly.] What was said by the person who broke the news to you? What was the first thing you said? What did you feel? What went on inside as it soaked in that it was really true? Did you want to scream? Want to hit somebody? Want to lie down and die? How did you think your family was going to respond? What about your friends? Or did you suddenly feel you were alone in your world with no one else? We are going to take three minutes of total silence as we hold hands, with our eyes closed. Remember.

The time may seem endless for some. Some may begin to cry. The leader has two tasks during the silence. He must keep the time, and he must try to get in touch with *his own loss*. He must be fully a part of everything going on. The group must learn that each person has the potential to become a "wounded healer."

At the end of the three minutes of silence, he will not be the first to share his feelings and memories unless no one else can muster up the courage to begin. But he must be prepared to share at least enough of himself to "prime the pump" for those who are too frightened and untrusting to reveal themselves with their own raw (and often embarrassing) feelings.

By the time the leader calls for attention, it is quite possible that someone will be crying. One person's tears may free others of their barriers. If many have fresh wounds, several may be crying. Whether several are crying or none, the leader will make the first opportunity a general one.

He will say something to the effect: "It is no longer necessary to hold hands. We have each had an opportunity to get in touch with our feelings about our losses. Several, if not most of us, are hurting to some degree right now. Who would like to be the first to share with us what is going on inside right now?"

By this time, the leader will have turned on all his sensors of emotion. He will be watching the eyes, the expressions about the mouth, the tightness of muscles in the face suggesting a clinched jaw, and for any other indicators of suppressed emotion. If no one speaks, we will look to the person whom he feels may be nearest to expressing himself and say something comparable to, "Mary, you've got something going on inside of you. Would you like to tell us something about it?"

If this person resists, he will immediately turn to some other person who seems close to expressing himself.

Only as a last resort will the leader begin to tell of his hurt. Even then, at the earliest opportunity, he will yield time to others in the group. One who has never hurt deeply is not yet mature enough to lead such a group.

Following Encounters

After the first session, meetings will usually begin with prayer and an inquiry into the well-being of members—especially those who have openly expressed themselves during the previous meeting. "What did you feel by the time you got home?" "What have you been thinking about during the past week that relates to what went on inside you last week?" Or the leader may note: "John, last week while Helen was talking I noticed something going on with you. Would you like to share that with us?"

Develop Leaders

People learn by observing and by doing. Look for an opportunity to develop leadership. Talk privately with any member of the group you recognize as having leadership potential about the possibility of preparing himself to lead a group at some time in the future. With encouragement and coaching, a participant can take more and more of a leadership role. This frees the original leader to pursue other important efforts.

Enlist New Members

Within the first three weeks, begin watching for new participants. This kind of group has the potential of going on and on. As members find healing, they move out and on to more pressing matters. Patients do not stay in the hospital after they have recovered their health. Others come in to take their place.

Enough is going on within the lives of the people of a church of three hundred active members to have a group that would be perpetuated for months or even for years.

I suggest you establish an operating procedure that within a week after the death of a member of the family of anyone in the church, the survivors would receive an explanation of what is going on in the loss recovery group and an invitation to participate in it. In addition, try to be alert to other losses. Talk personally with people who are retiring, those who are having to adjust their life-style because of health or loss of finances, those coming out of divorce, women who have had a mastectomy or hysterectomy, couples watching their last child leave home for college, or any other loss that commonly demands a painful adjustment.

Herein is an opportunity for the church to minister and promote healing for its body.

Notes

Chapter 1
1. Robert W. Bailey, *The Minister and Grief* (New York: Hawthorn Books, 1976), p. 47.

Chapter 2
1. *Newsweek,* May 1, 1978, p. 61.

Chapter 3
1. Erna Furman, *A Child's Parent Dies* (New Haven: Yale University Press, 1974), p. 15.
2. Ibid., p. 17.
3. Ibid., p. 20.
4. Ibid., p. 21.

Chapter 4
1. Robert W. Bailey, *The Minister and Grief* (New York: Hawthorn Books, 1976), p. 44 f.

Chapter 5
1. Charles C. Bachmann, *Ministering to the Grief Sufferer* (Englewood Cliffs: Prentice-Hall, 1964), pp. 127-129.
2. Edgar Jackson, *Understanding Grief* (Nashville, Abingdon Press, 1957), p. 90.
3. Quoted in William P. Tuck, *Facing Grief and Death* (Nashville: Broadman Press, 1975), p. 52.
4. William G. Justice, "A Matter of Confidence," *Church Administration,* vol. 19, no. 7 (April 1977), p. 26 ff.
5. Tuck, p. 60.
6. Thomas Fuller, in *The Encyclopedia of Religious Quotations,* ed. Frank S. Mead (Westwood, N. J.: Fleming H. Revell), p. 101.
7. Carl Boberg, tr. Stuart Hine, "How Great Thou Art," *Baptist*

Hymnal (Nashville: Convention Press, 1975), no. 35.

Appendix

1. Howard Clinebell, *Growth Groups* (Nashville: Abingdon Press, 1977), p. 112-114.

Recommended Readings

Bachmann, Charles C. *Ministering to the Grief Sufferer*. Englewood Cliffs: Prentice-Hall, 1964.

Bailey, Robert W. *The Minister and Grief*. New York: Hawthorn Books, 1976.

Booher, Dianna Daniels. *The Faces of Death*. Nashville: Broadman Press, 1980.

Brown, Velma Darbo. *After Weeping, A Song*. Nashville: Broadman Press, 1980.

_____. *A Fresh Look at Loneliness*. Nashville: Broadman Press, 1981.

Clark, George. *Thinking Ahead About Death*. Nashville: The Baptist Sunday School Board, 1979.

Claypool, John. *Tracks of a Fellow Struggler*. Waco: Word Books, 1974.

Clinebell, Howard. *Growth Groups*. Nashville: Abingdon Press, 1977.

Drakeford, John. *The Awesome Power of the Listening Ear*. Waco: Word Books, 1967.

Feifel, Herman. *The Meaning of Death*. New York: McGraw-Hill, 1959.

Furman, Erna. *A Child's Parent Dies*. New Haven and London: Yale University Press, 1974.

Irion, Paul E. *The Funeral: Vestige or Value?* Nashville: Abingdon Press, 1966.

Jackson, Edgar. *Understanding Grief*. Nashville: Abingdon Press, 1957.

_____. *Telling the Child About Death*. New York: Hawthorn Books, 1965.

————. *When Someone Dies.* Philadelphia: Fortress Press, 1971.

————. *The Many Faces of Grief.* Nashville: Abingdon Press, 1972.

Johnson, L. D. *The Morning After Death.* Nashville: Broadman Press, 1978.

McIntyre, J. Ralph. "After the Funeral," *Church Administration,* July 1979, p. 21 f.

Mitscherlich, Alexander and Margarete. *The Inability to Mourn.* New York: Grove Press, 1975.

Morris, Sarah. *Grief and How to Live With It.* New York: Grosset and Dunlap, 1972.

Oates, Wayne, Ed. *An Introduction to Pastoral Counseling.* Nashville: Broadman Press, 1959.

Schiff, Harriet Sarnoff. *The Bereaved Parent.* New York: Crown Publishers, 1977.

Switzer, David D. *The Dynamics of Grief.* Nashville: Abingdon Press, 1970.

Tuck, William P. *Facing Grief and Death.* Nashville: Broadman Press, 1975.

Westburg, Granger. *Good Grief.* Philadelphia: Fortress Press, 1961.